THE COMPLETE FILMS
OF
AUDREY HEPBURN

THE COMPLETE FILMS
OF
AUDREY
HEPBURN

JERRY VERMILYE

A CITADEL PRESS BOOK
Published by Carol Publishing Group

Carol Publishing Group Edition, 1998

A Citadel Press Book
Published by Carol Publishing Group
Citadel Press is a registered trademark of Carol Communications, Inc.

Editorial, sales and distribution, rights and permissions inquiries
should be addressed to Carol Publishing Group, 120 Enterprise Avenue,
Secaucus, N.J. 07094

In Canada: Canadian Manda Group, One Atlantic Avenue, Suite 105,
Toronto, Ontario M6K 3E7

Carol Publishing Group books may be purchased in bulk at special
discounts for sales promotions, fund-raising, or educational purposes.
Special editions can be created to specifications. For details, contact
Special Sales Department, Carol Publishing Group, 120 Enterprise Avenue,
Secaucus, N.J. 07094

Designed by A. Christopher Simon

Manufactured in the United States of America

10 9 8 7 6 5 4 3

Library of Congress Cataloging-in-Publication Data

Vermilye, Jerry.
    The complete films of Audrey Hepburn / Jerry Vermilye.
        p.   cm.
    "A Citadel Press book."
    ISBN 0-8065-1598-8 (pbk.)
    1. Hepburn, Audrey, 1929–   . I. Title.
PN2287.H43V47   1995
791.43'028'092—dc20   95-19766
                                              CIP

For
the Dibble sisters,
Connie, Judie, and Kitsy

And
for Donica

Acknowledgments

The author wishes to express his gratitude to the following individuals for giving so generously of their time to offer editorial assistance: Michael Buckley, Jim Butler, Judy Caputo, Bob Finn, Bill Grayson, David Hofstede, Gay Jordan, Alvin H. Marill, José Martinez, Jay Ogletree, Jim Prendergast, Thom Toney, Allan Turner, and the program UNICEF. And a salute to all of the anonymous still and portrait photographers whose artistry graces these pages, as well as to the companies that aired or distributed these films: Allied Artists, American Broadcasting Co., Associated British–Pathé, Columbia Pictures, Corona, Eros, Favorite Pictures, General Film Distributors, Lippert Pictures, Metro-Goldwyn-Mayer, Moon Pictures, Paramount Pictures, Stratford Pictures, Twentieth Century-Fox, United Artists, Universal Pictures, and Warner Brothers.

Contents

THE WOMAN

Portrait (1953)

Audrey Hepburn

Audrey Hepburn. More than two years after her untimely death at sixty-three, her name alone continues to evoke smiles of affection, words of admiration—and continued interest even after the many books and publications about her. In a career whose peak years nearly paralleled those of Marilyn Monroe, Hepburn uniquely balanced the appearance of that charismatic blonde with a darker, quieter beauty marked by grace, style, and a simple elegance that didn't prevent her easily slipping into gamine roles. While Marilyn was physically curvaceous, Audrey was tall, slim, and boyish of figure with big, mesmerizing doe-eyes and a warm, winning smile that more than compensated for any physical shortcomings. Both stars were influential in their style and in their attire, and each was sexy in her own particular way, appealing—nonthreateningly—to women, as well as men. Most of the great movie stars have their partisans as well as detractors, but with Audrey Hepburn it is difficult to find negative comments. During her years as a working actress, the press sometimes criticized her vehicles, but seldom her. On the whole, it seemed that she could do no wrong. Her slight but hard-to-place accent (which many at first took for British), carefully enunciated in a velvety purr, only served to underscore her continental sophistication. With her ballet-bred posture and five-foot-seven frame, it was only natural that she would adapt easily to high-fashion clothing—and that Hubert de Givenchy would become her favorite designer, as well as a lifelong friend.

At twenty-four, Audrey Hepburn suddenly became an "overnight" sensation in *Roman Holiday*. It was her first starring part but her eighth motion picture. Her entire career would encompass only nineteen more theatrical films and two made-for-television features—a slim filmography, very much on a par with the motion picture legacies of Monroe and Garbo. And, as with those beloved stars, it appears likely that Audrey's legend will prevail and endure as long as motion pictures are preserved on film, laser disc, and videocassette.

"I'm not a born actress, as such, but I care about expressing feelings," she told an interviewer in 1987, while making the television movie *Love Among Thieves*. Then facing the prospect of returning to show business for the first time in seven years, she had initially informed that film's director, Roger Young, that she "couldn't act" and would need "lots of help." Those were sentiments that she modestly echoed—against strong protests from interviewer Richard

Portrait (1953)

Portrait (1954)

Brown—when the star sat for a retrospective career appraisal for American Movie Classics on cable television.

"I was born with something that appealed to an audience at that particular time," she told Brown, with analytic modesty. "I acted instinctively. I've had one of the greatest schools of all—a whole row of great, great directors." Along with her fresh-scrubbed natural beauty, Hepburn's utter lack of pretense and easy admission of her sixty-odd years only further endeared her to those for whom she would always remain their "fair lady," to echo a term destined for repetition in her press memorials. For the wondrous magic of the screen is that time cannot alter what has been captured there: One will always have her inimitable interpretations of Princess Anne, Sabrina Fairchild, Natasha Rostov, Jo Stockton, Ariane Chavasse, Sister Luke, Holly Golightly, Karen Wright, Reggie Lambert, Eliza Doolittle, Joanna Wallace, Susy Hendrix, and Maid Marian, among others, to charm and enchant them all over again.

But Audrey Hepburn was never comfortable in the guise of a glamorous movie star. "I never understood what makes me so special," she once remarked. And she added, "That was a job, not reality."

In so-called "middle age," when suitable roles became increasingly harder to find, she chose to withdraw from films and channel her energy on domesticity and motherhood, until such time as a movie offer might engage her interest.

At an age (fifty-nine) when most semiretired movie actresses are content to take life easier, she agreed to become a UNICEF Special Ambassador, which involved traveling as spokesperson for suffering third-world children. It has been said that "Goodwill Ambassador" was Audrey Hepburn's greatest role.

She was born Andrey Kathleen Ruston on May 4, 1929, in Brussels, Belgium. But this unusual form of the masculine Andrew would often result in her name being misspelled "Audrey." Because of her heritage (Dutch on her mother's side, British on her father's), the child's nationality was officially British. Her

Portrait (1956)

Portrait (1959)

twice-divorced mother, the aristocratic Baroness Ella van Heemstra, already had two sons from her first marriage when she met and wed Joseph Victor Henry Ruston, a divorced Briton who was with the diplomatic service as vice consul in the Netherlands East Indies, where they were married in 1926. The name Hepburn-Ruston was manufactured by the baroness, who selected the Hepburn part from her husband's family tree, because she liked its noble sound. But the hyphenated name was never legalized and was used only for appearances.

By the time of Audrey's birth, the Hepburn-Rustons had moved from primitive Java to London and, finally, to Brussels, where Ruston managed a branch office of an Anglo-French credit firm. The baby's half brothers, Alexander and Ian Quarles van Ufford, were then eight and four years her senior, respectively. Not unexpectedly, she grew up closer to Ian, developing into a shy but mischievous tomboy.

From an early age, Audrey was multilingual and conversant in English, French, Dutch, and Flemish.

Portrait (1959)

Portrait with "Mr. Famous" (1959)

with the other girls. Deprived of her mother's presence, Audrey withdrew into herself and took to overeating and nail-biting. The baroness, meanwhile, moved back to Holland with her sons, settling on her parents' handsome estate in Arnhem, where she resumed the name Ella van Heemstra. But it became necessary for her to spend periods of time in England with Audrey, in order to bring the child out of her proverbial shell. And by her second year at the school, Audrey had made friends with some of her classmates and discovered the world of dance through the teachings of a Miss Rigden, who was greatly influenced by Isadora Duncan. The baroness was informed that,

Portrait (1966)

But all was not serene in the Hepburn-Ruston home; her parents quarreled constantly, and, sometime after her sixth birthday, in May 1935, Joseph Ruston walked out on his family and didn't return. Already an introverted child, Audrey now realized a sense of loss and insecurity that would follow her throughout her life, for she adored her father. Years later, Audrey would admit that his departure caused "one of the traumas that left a very deep mark on me."

The resultant divorce stipulated that young Audrey be educated near London, for her father's visitation benefit. And so, with Ella's consent, their daughter was enrolled in a small private school in the Kentish village of Elham, where she found it difficult to mix

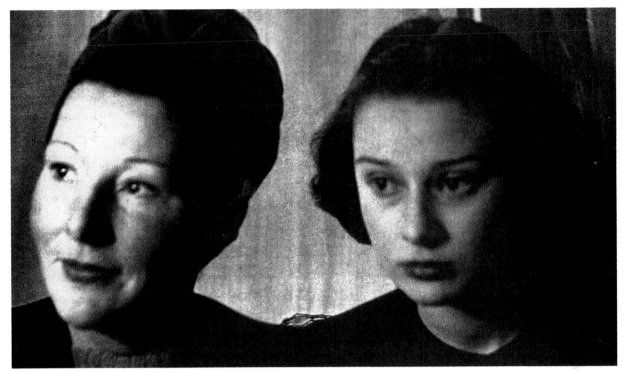

At seventeen with her mother in 1946

should Audrey get the right training, the girl might have a future in ballet.

By Audrey's tenth birthday, in the spring of 1939, the world situation had changed considerably. At first it was thought advisable to keep her in England. But when both France and Great Britain declared war against Germany that September, the baroness moved to bring Audrey home, since Holland was neutral. She left England on one of the last planes out, parting from her father for what would be a separation of many years.

Back in the Netherlands, living in Arnhem proved safer, for a time, but it also challenged Audrey, when she entered the local school system, to become more proficient in Dutch. She continued to pursue her intense interest in dance and became a student at the Arnhem Conservatory of Music. But in May of 1940, Germany invaded Holland, and Audrey's studies and lifestyle were disrupted. The next four years were difficult, and she usually avoided talking about them in later years. During the Occupation, food was often hard to obtain, with the result that Audrey became very thin and anemic. Identity cards were required of anyone fifteen or older and were stamped with a prominent "J" if the bearer was Jewish. But the van Heemstras were spared that fate because, although

With fellow chorus aspirant Babs Johnston at *High Button Shoes* auditions in 1948

19

the family bore Jewish blood in their ancestry, it was apparently too far back to gain the attention of the Nazis. However, much of their property was confiscated, and the baroness had to leave the van Heemstra mansion for a modest flat over the shops in central Arnhem, because their home was appropriated by Nazi officers. To protect Audrey, the baroness forbade her to speak English, and to keep the Germans from singling her out, the girl was henceforth to be known only as Edda van Heemstra, thus concealing her mixed parentage. Audrey's father, meanwhile, was incarcerated by the British government as a security risk because of his profascist sympathies. He would spend much of the war's duration in a detention camp on the Isle of Man.

Like many children in the midst of war, Audrey found mental escape in her dance classes at the conservatory, while her half brother Alexander, who had joined the Dutch army at the time of the German invasion, went into hiding to avoid imprisonment by the enemy. In 1942, tragedy struck the family when Audrey's uncle, Otto van Limburg Stirum, was executed, along with four other prominent men, as reprisal for an act of sabotage by the Dutch Resistance. In the summer of 1943 her half brother Ian was among the local young men rounded up and thrown into a German labor camp. To aid the Resistance, Audrey danced with her classmates in fund-raising evenings, performed in secret behind black-curtained windows. As she later recalled, "We danced to scratchy old recordings of highlights from *Swan Lake*, *The Nutcracker*, and *Giselle*, which has always been my favorite among the classical ballets." And she admitted, "I always had to be the boy in a pas de deux, because I was too tall to play the girl."

At fifteen, in 1944, Audrey appeared with other students at Arnhem's municipal theater in a recital that won her special attention from a magazine critic, who wrote, "She seems obsessed by a real dance rage, and already has a respectable technical proficiency."

Her ingenuous appearance cast Audrey as now-and-then courier for the Resistance, carrying forged ration cards and false identity papers, which students often hid in their schoolbags. On one such occasion, she witnessed Nazis herding Jewish families into railroad cars, undoubtedly bound for the death camps. Finally, on the morning of September 17, 1944, came the massive Allied offensive known as Operation Market Garden, in which aircraft arrived from England to combat the Nazi defenses and gain control of the now celebrated "bridge too far" that crossed the Rhine into Germany. Because the enemy knew in advance of those plans, the ensuing battle lasted a lengthy ten days, resulting in what historians have claimed were more Allied casualties than racked up by the D-day invasion of Normandy. In retaliation for the Dutch Resistance's role in this carnage, the Nazis devastated much of Arnhem, including the Conservatory of Music, and the populace was ordered to evacuate the city within twenty-four hours. Audrey and her mother left on foot, walking the five miles to Grandpa van Heemstra's home in Velp. As Audrey later recalled, "It was human misery at its starkest. Masses of refugees on the move, some carrying their dead; babies born on the roadside; hundreds collapsing of hunger."

It was during this period that malnutrition is reported to have permanently damaged Audrey's metabolism, initiating a lifelong mission to gain weight, as well as erroneous rumors of anorexia in years to come.

Audrey's sixteenth birthday—May 4, 1945—was more than proverbially "sweet," with the liberation of the Netherlands. For Arnhem, it was Canadian troops who were the liberators, and Audrey recalled, "We whooped and hollered and danced for joy. I wanted to kiss every one of them. The incredible relief of being free—it's something that's hard to verbalize. Freedom is more like something in the air. For me, it was hearing soldiers speaking English instead of German, and smelling real tobacco smoke again from their cigarettes."

Rallying to the war-torn Dutch citizenry were the International Red Cross and the United Nations Relief Agency, with their food and their medicines. And then came the much appreciated CARE packages, as Arnhem gradually came back to life. Both of Audrey's half brothers survived the war: Ian returned home from Berlin, mostly on foot; and Alexander, who had wed a local girl, made Audrey an aunt. Concerned about her father, she sought assistance from the International Red Cross and eventually learned that he was alive and living in Ireland. Though relieved, she also felt abandoned: "I didn't try to reach him. By then the war had been over for months and he had never tried to reach *me*, nor had I ever heard from him in the ten months between my leaving England and Holland's occupation. So the feelings of rejection were very strong, and I thought he didn't want to see me anymore." What she didn't know then was

In the London revue *Sauce Tartare* in 1949

Audrey free lessons, since she realized there was no money for such a luxury. A month later, the baroness tired of housekeeping for others and found a position as manager of a florist shop—and a flat that she could share with her daughter. Audrey continued to study with Gaskell, who proved an excellent motivator for the girl as well as an excellent teacher. And, in interpreting dance, the enthusiastic pupil also showed a marked talent for acting. In a May 1946 recital of Gaskell students at Amsterdam's Hortus Theatre, she won the notice of a critic from *Algemeen Handelsblad*, who wrote of the seventeen-year-old, who was now calling herself Audrey Hepburn, "She does not yet have much technique, but she is undoubtedly talented."

Dance now meant everything to Audrey, and although she never completed the schooling that had been cut short in wartime Arnhem, she continued to

that, during the war, he had not been *able* to contact her, and that he was now in ill health and penniless, depending on the charity of Trappist monks in County Waterford.

With the war over, the baroness turned her attentions to her daughter, whose talents mandated that they continue the ballet training that had been interrupted by war. But the van Heemstra fortunes were now gone, necessitating that employment be sought. The city of Amsterdam appeared a more likely prospect for their future, and the baroness managed to secure a live-in housekeeping position there, taking Audrey with her. The girl found lodgings at the home of her new dance teacher, Sonia Gaskell, who offered

In the London revue *Sauce Piquante* in 1950

As a young London model

land and its highlights. With the casting of professional actor Wam Heskes to portray that part (and narrate), it was decided to hire nonprofessionals for those he encounters along the way. Audrey applied for the silent role of a KLM airline stewardess, whose only requirement was to be "pretty." Producer van der Linden later remembered Audrey's interview, in which she could only tell him about her dance background. But he was immediately charmed: "Audrey was bright, cheerful, chummy, and just emanated style, breeding, intelligence, and good manners." She tested in her best dress, accessoried by a fussy hat and long gloves—and won the role. They even recycled her screen test as part of the movie's opening sequence. A supporting-length feature, *Nederlands in zeven lessen* won no personal notices for Audrey Hepburn and wasn't seen outside of the Netherlands.

In an MGM costume test for *Quo Vadis*

study ballet. Her mother, meanwhile, now worked in a beauty salon, where, to help finance her dance instruction, the girl made hats for sale to the baroness's customers. And then, suddenly, Sonia Gaskell was forced to close her studio and seek funding elsewhere. Audrey had heard about the possibility of a scholarship to study with the famed ballerina Marie Rambert in London, and while she and her mother strived to get through the red tape that might make it possible, she sought money for her dance lessons by applying for a bit role in a 1948 film called *Nederlands in zeven lessen*. It was originally planned as a travel short for Britain's Rank Organisation. But the original financing had collapsed, and Dutch filmmakers Hein Josephson and Charles van der Linden were left with endless aerial footage of the Netherlands on their hands. To answer the question of what to do with it, they devised a film-within-a-film about a cameraman who is given seven days to photograph Hol-

22

As Gigi in her Broadway debut (1951)

Director van der Linden laments the Dutch film industry's failure to continue grooming Hepburn for their own screen: "I definitely thought she had something special. She radiated sunshine. I wanted to make a starring film with her, but I couldn't raise the financing, and we both moved on to other things. Audrey Hepburn was the superstar who got away."

Audrey next found part-time employment as a fashion-salon mannequin for Tonny Waagemans, whose widow remembers Audrey at nineteen: "She had a natural elegance. She was a real personality, and she walked beautifully. When we had our mode shows, Audrey was always the model who got the most applause."

With the bureaucratic path now cleared for Audrey to study ballet with Rambert in London, she and her mother finalized immigration requirements and finally left for Britain on December 18, 1948. They first found bed-and-breakfast lodgings in London, then visited Rambert, for whom she had to display her practice techniques. The result was only a partial scholarship by which her new student would receive free tuition, but nothing further; she would have to support herself.

A stern disciplinarian, Marie Rambert didn't make student life easy for Audrey Hepburn, who was deemed too tall to ever become a solo ballerina, as was her dearest wish. "I tried to do whatever I could for her," Rambert remembered. "She was a good worker, a wonderful learner. I always knew she would amount to something, but there was no future for her in my company of dancers. Even in classes, it was always a struggle to find partners who were tall enough for her."

Audrey and her mother shared a Bayswater bed-sitter, while the baroness found it impossible, as a resident alien, to obtain a work permit. Illegally, however, she managed to make friends with someone in the decorating business, then induced a well-heeled acquaintance to name her manager of an apartment house that he owned in fashionable Mayfair. Their agreement allowed her a flat in the building but no salary, so Audrey took on part-time office jobs, for which she had time after her dance classes. The association with Marie Rambert also led to modeling jobs, for which her long-limbed slimness made her ideal. And in doing so, she learned about clothes and what styles and colors best suited her.

The Hepburn face first became known to the British people through print ads for a beauty product called Lacto-Calamine, whose slogan was "A powder base by day, a skin food by night." Since this aspect of show business brought her income, however small, she gave some thought to London's theater world—outside of ballet. Especially unsettling for Audrey was the knowledge that not only was her height a handicap, but also she would need at least five more years of concentrated dance study to meet the requirements of the profession. However, since some of her classmates regularly answered London casting calls for jobs in the somewhat less demanding areas of nightclubs and vaudeville, she began to audition with

her friends. The nostalgic American musical *High Button Shoes*, a Broadway hit in 1947, was casting for the dancing chorus, and she applied, although, as she later admitted, "I knew nothing about modern dance steps, and my ear wasn't attuned to the rhythms. I don't know how I even had the nerve to try for the job in the first place."

But her wide-eyed charm and her dance training attracted the attention of director Archie Thomson, and she was hired for eight pounds a week. It opened at Christmastime 1948 and kept the scarcely billed Audrey Hepburn busy for a while, especially in the frantic "Mack Sennett Ballet," in which Keystone Kops pursued bathing beauties and others around the boardwalk in Atlantic City—all of which was choreographed to a turn by Jerome Robbins at his most inventive. One night, visiting showman Cecil Landeau attended *High Button Shoes* and was captured by Audrey's vivacity: "Something projected over the footlights. I marked her down in my book as someone to consider when I started casting my next production."

That opportunity came more quickly than expected

With her mentor Cathleen Nesbitt in *Gigi* (1951)

when *High Button Shoes* fell victim to a sagging box office and suddenly closed. In need of income, Audrey decided against continuing with Marie Rambert and determined to refocus her performing sights: "I was finally earning money as a dancer. Maybe it wasn't the kind of dancing I dreamed of, but I was out of the classroom and into the real world. I loved being in a musical show. For the first time, I felt the pure joy of living."

Cecil Landeau remembered her from *High Button Shoes* and hired her for the chorus of his 1949 revue *Sauce Tartare*, which utilized her talents in musical numbers and comedy sketches. It was a hit, and Audrey was bringing in ten pounds per week. The show led to additional modeling jobs and even an interview with Metro-Goldwyn-Mayer, among other film studios. But nothing came of those possibilities, and she stayed with *Sauce Tartare* for a run of 437 performances at the Cambridge Theatre. It was closely followed by Landeau's next revue, *Sauce Piquante*, which opened in April 1950. This time, while continuing as a chorus girl, Audrey Hepburn also got to introduce skits and speak lines, and she was now paid twelve pounds a week. Bob Monkhouse, who was among the show's featured comics, remembers her not being a very good dancer, yet attracting undue audience interest, nevertheless. Analyzing her magic, he said, "What Audrey had was an enormous, exaggerated feeling of 'I need you.' Judy Garland always had that; the message was urgent: 'I'm helpless—I need you.' When people sense this, they respond to it immediately, perhaps not realizing why they're doing so. And Audrey had it in abundance, that same air of defenselessness, helplessness. I think everybody in the audience thought, 'I want to look after little Audrey.' She seemed to be too pretty, too unaware of the dangers of life."

Cecil Landeau now appeared to take a special interest in Audrey Hepburn, thinking to move her out of the chorus and into an acting lead for his next *Sauce* revue. And so he arranged for her to study with character actor Felix Aylmer, who was responsible for polishing her British accent and lowering its rather high pitch.

Sauce Piquante failed to enjoy the success of its predecessor, but before it closed, twenty-one-year-old Audrey experienced her first romance—with one of the revue's stars, a French singer named Marcel Le Bon, who courted her with red roses. Cecil Landeau disapproved of their relationship and tried to discourage it, claiming that his audiences wanted his showgirls to be unattached. After *Sauce Piquante*'s demise, Landeau dumped Le Bon and staged a condensed version of the revue, this time entitled *Summer Nights*, which he turned into a floor show for Ciro's nightclub. Again, Audrey Hepburn was featured in the cast, and again she caught the attention of audiences more for her personality than for her talents. Indeed, a casting agent for Associated British Pictures noticed her there and recommended her to director Mario Zampi, who was seeking a young actress for a leading role in his comedy *Laughter in Paradise*. But Audrey was in love, and she turned down the movie opportunity, because she and Le Bon (of whom her mother the baroness strongly disapproved) were hoping to team for a nightclub tour. Their relationship eventually broke apart when Le Bon's plans fell through, ending with his accepting engagements in Canada and the United States. When Audrey contacted Zampi to advise him of her new availability, she discovered that her role had gone to Beatrice Campbell. All that he could now offer her was a cigarette-girl bit in a nightclub scene. She took it.

Through her first agent, Jack Dunfee of Linnit and Dunfee, Audrey found other small-part employment in early-fifties pictures, among them *One Wild Oat*, starring Robertson Hare and Stanley Holloway, and *The Lavender Hill Mob*, in which she shared one brief scene—and the single line "Oh, but how sweet of you! Thank you!" with no less than Britain's then-favorite film actor, Alec Guinness. In *Young Wives' Tale*, however, she enjoyed a more substantial supporting role, as well as scenes with that 1951 comedy's stars, Joan Greenwood, Nigel Patrick, and Derek Farr. But she later recalled this as her least favorite movie experience, due to the ongoing disapproval of director Henry Cass, who, she said, "had it in for me!"

At a party following completion of the movie, Audrey first met James Hanson, the twenty-eight-year-old scion of a wealthy trucking executive. He was known as a debonair playboy associated with posh cars, nightclubs, and beautiful actresses. Hanson and Audrey Hepburn immediately became an "item." And while he maintained a hectic business schedule, often involving trips to Canada, she continued to toil in the London film studios. She even caught the eye of Hollywood's Mervyn LeRoy, who tested her for *Quo Vadis*. The director was interested in using her for

On location in Rome for *Roman Holiday* in 1952 with director William Wyler and costar Gregory Peck

With fiancé James Hanson

the role of Lygia in his Roman-spectacle drama, but MGM insisted on a name actress, and the part went to Deborah Kerr.

Audrey then won her most substantial role to date, as the young-dancer sister of Valentina Cortesa in director Thorold Dickinson's *Secret People*, a dramatic story of European-born political terrorists in London. And although some credulity was strained by Cortesa's Italian accent next to Hepburn's British one, there was believability in her ballet scenes, which involved barre practice and the performance of a white-wigged dance, in which she was partnered by the Royal Ballet's John Field. The scene took two full days of filming a sequence that had already been rehearsed for nine more, and it proved so painful an experience that Audrey welcomed the acting scenes. In her first big movie role, her lack of technique was bolstered by her director, who knew just how to get the best out of a nervous newcomer. "Don't bother about how you're going to play the scene or recite the lines," Dickinson advised her. "Think of the emotion behind the words. Try connecting them to something you've felt in your own life. If you get the feeling right, everything else will take care of itself."

By this time, she and James Hanson were thinking about marriage, with Audrey considering giving up what little career she might have for domesticity. The baroness, impressed with Hanson's background, which included a beautiful Yorkshire estate, approved of this match, especially as she didn't much care for what she had thus far seen of London show business.

Ealing Studios liked Hepburn's performance in their *Secret People* sufficiently to give her third billing—albeit in smaller lettering—after Valentina Cortesa and Serge Reggiani. But the film was considered too arty for popular consumption, and it did little to attract interest in Audrey. She was up for the young lead in a comedy called *Lady Godiva Rides Again*, but was deemed too thin for the requisite bathing suit, and the role went to Pauline Stroud—who went nowhere. Ealing writer-producer Alfred Shaughnessy liked her work in *Secret People* and wanted her for his *Brandy for the Parson*. However, Associated British had just assigned her to a comedy to be alternately filmed in French and English (as *Monte Carlo Baby*) on the Riviera.

Audrey's presence at the Hotel de Paris for filming on a certain afternoon would have a fateful impact on her future, when she caught the eye of the legendary French writer Colette, who was a guest there. For two days, Audrey noticed the elderly novelist in her wheelchair, attended by her husband Maurice Goudeket, watching the film being shot. Eventually, she was summoned to their suite and informed that Mme. Colette believed the young actress might be just the person to portray the title role in her *Gigi* in its forthcoming stage adaptation that was scheduled for presentation on Broadway. The writer had even gone so far as to cable its American adaptor, Anita Loos: "Don't cast your Gigi until you receive my letter."

Responding to the blandishments of Mme. Colette—who gushed, "You are my Gigi! You have that piquant quality so essential to the part. Would you not like to do it?"—Audrey weighed the offer before replying, "I'm sorry, Madame, but I wouldn't be able to, because I can't act. I'm not equipped to play a leading role. I've never said more than one or two lines on stage in my life. I've done bits in films, of course, but I don't consider that acting."

But the writer refused to take no for an answer,

expressing her faith in Audrey Hepburn's dance background: "If you've been a dancer, you must have worked hard, and if you work hard, you can do this, too."

Reading the book *Gigi* during the completion of *Monte Carlo Baby*, Audrey entertained further doubts about her ability to pass for a sixteen-year-old schoolgirl in turn-of-the-century Paris who is being groomed by her relatives to become a courtesan in the family tradition. Ultimately, the girl finds true love and marriage to the very libertine selected to be her protector. Colette's popular novella had first been published in 1944 in Switzerland and had enjoyed success in a 1946 English translation. Daniele Delorme had played the character in a 1948 French film, and there would be an Oscar-winning MGM musical version, starring Leslie Caron, in 1958. But, before that, there was Audrey Hepburn, making her American debut on the stage in *Gigi*. Out-of-town previews began on November 8, 1951, in Philadelphia, and the production opened, produced by Gilbert Miller and directed

Performing a scene from *Anne of the Thousand Days* with Rex Harrison on Ed Sullivan's *Toast of the Town* TV show

At the *Roman Holiday* premiere with Irving Berlin (*left*) and Paramount production chief Don Hartman in 1953

Holiday screenplay, and then, when Audrey thought the cameras were finished, she reacted naturally with a few words of relief and a girlish laugh that Dickinson managed to catch on film. Wyler was suitably charmed and offered her the role, although preparations for *Gigi* appeared to conflict—until Gregory Peck had to postpone *Roman Holiday* for the completion of *The Snows of Kilimanjaro*. Hepburn's availability now hinged on the future of *Gigi*. Paramount was willing to take a chance on her, but since hers was not yet a famous name, they urged her to change it to avoid public confusion with *Katharine* Hepburn. On the grounds that the obvious age difference would hardly see them in competition for the same roles, Audrey refused.

The Philadelphia critics had been mixed in their reactions to *Gigi*. But there was no lack of agreement about Audrey Hepburn; two papers called her "the acting find of the year," and *Variety*'s man on the aisle wrote, "Miss Hepburn has real talent as well as a magnetic personality." By the time the play reached Broadway, Audrey had caught the flu. At the opening performance, her strength was ebbing by the play's last scene. In her own words: "I forgot my lines and

by Raymond Rouleau, at New York's Fulton Theatre (later renamed the Helen Hayes, before its 1982 demolition) less than one month later, on November 24. It had taken a lot of work—as Mme. Colette herself had predicted—to get her there, and the coaching of the veteran actress Cathleen Nesbitt (who played Gigi's worldly Aunt Alicia) to perfect Audrey's inadequate natural vocal projection. Hers was a run-of-the-play contract that paid her five hundred dollars a week, minus agent's fees and living expenses, for she was still an "unknown quantity" so far as Broadway was concerned.

Before leaving London for New York, Audrey Hepburn had been tested for the female lead in William Wyler's *Roman Holiday*, a Paramount production already set to star Gregory Peck. She was among five British actresses being tested, and had the good fortune to have her footage directed by *Secret People*'s Thorold Dickinson. They shot pages from the *Roman*

Reunited in Hoboken, New Jersey, with her mother, Baroness Ella van Heemstra, after a two-year separation (1953)

28

everything stopped. I missed a whole speech, but somehow I backtracked and the audience didn't seem to notice. I prayed for a miracle before I went on that night, and I think that I got it."

Her Broadway opening brought the baroness and James Hanson over from London, and they witnessed not only three solo curtain calls for Audrey, but also a standing ovation—a decided rarity in 1951. With many more dailies then than now, the New York critics were split as to the play's merits (three were favorable; five were negative), but nearly all found praise for Audrey Hepburn. In the *New York Times*, Brooks Atkinson called her "a young actress of charm, honesty and talent who ought to be interned in America and trapped into appearing in a fine play." Walter Kerr, writing in the *New York Herald-Tribune*, said, "She brings a candid innocence and a tomboy intelligence to a part that might have gone sticky, and her performance comes like a breath of fresh air in a stifling season." Producer Gilbert Miller's reaction was to give his new leading lady star billing: The marquee would henceforth proclaim

"AUDREY HEPBURN in *GIGI*."

Gigi quickly became a sold-out Broadway hit, while Miller and playwright Loos tried to negotiate a motion picture deal for the play—and Audrey. But in the early fifties, Hollywood wasn't ready to handle such risqué material.

Audrey was now stuck with a hit and could only hope to see James Hanson on her days off. But their love appeared secure, despite her theatrical commitment, and after he had presented her with a diamond ring, their engagement became official. That, plus her new recognition as a Broadway star, increased Audrey's visibility and made her a vulnerable press target. She hated that. With Cathleen Nesbitt continuing to coach her, Audrey now considered herself "halfway between a dancer and an actress," and she credited her ballet training with giving her the stamina to survive eight live performances a week.

The success of *Gigi* now worried Paramount, for producer Miller was considering extending the play's run into the summer, which might have precluded her availability for *Roman Holiday*. Problems were smoothed over by the movie company, which paid Miller $50,000 for Hepburn's release in late May, with the proviso that she be finished with the picture in time to rejoin *Gigi* for its road tour later in the

year. Consequently, the play closed on May 24, 1952, after a run of 217 performances, and Audrey made preparations for her big movie break. She and Hanson now planned to wed as soon as *Roman Holiday* was completed.

It's difficult to believe that anyone could have portrayed the film's heroine, Princess Anne, any better than Audrey Hepburn. It had earlier been considered for Elizabeth Taylor, then Jean Simmons, before Audrey's casting. All about the romantic idyll of a royal miss from an unnamed European country who meets an American journalist when she runs away from her state duties during a tour of Rome, the story follows their whirlwind fling (innocent of sexual dalliance in 1953), from chance meeting to bittersweet parting. In the final scene, as she meets with the world's press, the lovers experience an anticlimactic farewell in the stiff formality of their professional real-life roles. Produced on location in the Eternal City, *Roman Holiday* had everything but Technicolor. Its teaming of Hepburn and Peck was so congenial that the actor demanded that Audrey receive secondary billing, equal in size to his own, rather than the planned "introducing Audrey Hepburn," to follow the title in smaller letters. And in William Wyler, she was equally blessed with a director who knew how to get the best out of his stars. In fact, Wyler was reportedly unusually kind and considerate of Hepburn—up until they shot the emotional farewell between her and Peck. The actress has told of how they tried and tried to get it right, but that no tears would come—until Wyler became exasperated, completely lost his patience, and berated her so severely that she burst into sobs, and they quickly shot the scene again, this time with success.

As Peck has told interviewers, "Everyone on the set fell in love with her"—which would explain why the notoriously difficult Wyler turned pussycat on the set of *Roman Holiday*. He and Audrey Hepburn would work together on two subsequent pictures over the ensuing thirteen years. "You could *believe* Audrey as a princess," said her director. "Even if you had never seen her before, and she walked into a room, you would have assumed that she was one."

Filming kept her busy until October, with no opportunity for a vacation before returning to New York for *Gigi*'s road tour, an engagement that would keep her busy through the first quarter of 1953. During the play's Chicago engagement, she was joined by her fiancé, who flew over from London to celebrate Christmas with her. Their reunion was quiet and private, but it ended with a formal announcement to the effect that their engagement had been broken. Audrey's official stand was that, since she was also very much in love with her profession, "it would be unfair to marry Jimmy." She informed a columnist that she had no wish to humiliate him by making him a "Mr. Audrey Hepburn." As for the former object of her affections, he would survive their breakup to eventually become the billionaire owner of Hanson PLC, long married to one woman and the father of three.

After *Gigi* finally closed in San Francisco that spring of 1953, Audrey flew off to London for a reunion with the baroness and the vacation she had long needed. Since Gregory Peck was then shooting *Night People* in Europe, Paramount arranged to welcome her by getting their stars back together for a big cocktail party. It was there that Audrey was introduced to Peck's friend, actor Mel Ferrer, who was in London to film *Knights of the Round Table*. She told the actor how much she had liked his work in the recent *Lili*, and they enjoyed talking theater.

As Ferrer later remembered, "We talked vaguely about doing a play together, and she asked me to send her a likely script if I found one." Despite a twelve-year age gap between them, their mutual attraction was pronounced and immediate. During her London stay, Audrey accompanied the actor to the theater on several occasions, but she was well aware that he was a married man with children.

Paramount, which had set *Roman Holiday*'s world premiere for New York's Radio City Music Hall, knew in advance that they had a potential superstar on their hands, and they secured rights to an incoming Broadway romantic comedy called *Sabrina Fair*, written by Samuel Taylor and set to star Margaret Sullavan as the Long Island chauffeur's daughter who blooms into a Cinderella and gets her choice of two wealthy suitors. Billy Wilder was set to direct Hepburn in the movie. Meanwhile, *Roman Holiday* opened to sensational notices, enthusiastic audiences, and a raft of publicity generated not only by Paramount publicists but also by the journalistic tycoons who fell victim to the inescapable fresh charms of Audrey Hepburn herself. Seemingly overnight, the whole world appeared to embrace this new screen enchantress, and if she was the flavor of the moment in Britain

and America, she was the absolute toast of Japan. Interestingly, a 1990 Japanese poll revealed that *Roman Holiday* (closely followed by *Gone With the Wind*) was that country's all-time favorite foreign film.

The filming of *Sabrina* (as *Sabrina Fair* was called in the U.S.) was a somewhat less pleasurable experience for Audrey Hepburn. Of her two leading men, Humphrey Bogart—for reasons of his own—proved the more difficult to find rapport with, especially since he openly disliked Wilder and had little use for William Holden. The latter, however, was a Wilder favorite, already having given two of his best performances in the director's *Sunset Boulevard* and *Stalag 17*. The handsome, married actor also fast became a Hepburn favorite during *Sabrina*'s production, and it has been reported that they spent a lot of time together, both on and off the set.

Sabrina is also notable for introducing Audrey to the man with whose designs she would become indelibly associated—Hubert de Givenchy, a couturier often known merely by his last name. Although Paramount's "house" designer, Edith Head, was set to create the star's *Sabrina* wardrobe, as she had done for *Roman Holiday*, Billy Wilder seriously damaged her ego by sending Audrey to the young French designer recommended by his wife, who had discovered him during a European shopping trip. Told to expect "Miss Hepburn" from the States, Givenchy has admitted his chagrin upon first meeting not the famed Katharine, but a tall, dark, and unfamiliar young lady, whose natural charm soon melted away his disappointment and initiated a lifelong friendship. For *Sabrina*, Audrey selected an off-the-shoulder, black-and-white evening dress that created a sensation. And if Edith Head was less than pleased, at least her revenge was sweet: Since hers was *Sabrina*'s official credit for costume design, its eventual Academy Award went, not to Givenchy, but to Edith Head!

Hepburn's next career move took her away from Hollywood and William Holden (reportedly, he was more serious than she) and back to New York, where Mel Ferrer, true to his word, had found in Jean Giraudoux's *Ondine* a stage vehicle for them both. It was a romantic fantasy, based on an old German legend, about a medieval knight and a water nymph. The fairy tale had already been the inspiration for no fewer than two nineteenth-century German operas, both entitled *Undine*. With Maurice Valency creating the English adaptation and Alfred Lunt directing,

Going over her script of
Ondine with Mel Ferrer

Ondine opened at New York's Forty-sixth Street Theatre (now the Richard Rodgers) on February 18, 1954,
and ran for 157 performances.

It was Audrey who had insisted that Mel, as her
costar, share equal billing with her, as they also
shared the curtain calls—much to the chagrin of those
who wished to worship Audrey Hepburn alone. Re-
hearsals for the play had not gone without backstage
incident, since Ferrer's influence on his leading lady
frequently appeared to exclude Lunt. Understandably, talk about a Trilby-Svengali relationship arose
from this production, amid veiled accusations that
Mel was simply using Audrey to elevate his own
flagging career as an actor-director.

But the Hepburn-Ferrer relationship grew during
Ondine's preparations, with the result that they began
sharing quarters in an apartment the actress had sub-
let in Greenwich Village. News of their liaison moti-
vated his wife, Frances, to seek a divorce.

Ondine received some glowing notices for Audrey
(the *New York Times* called her "magical" and "rap-
turously beautiful"), but less acclaim for Mel. But

With Mel Ferrer in Broadway's *Ondine* in 1954

In Broadway's *Ondine* (1954)

In Broadway's *Ondine* (1954)

Audrey truly reached her pinnacle as a triumphant young actress during the week of March 25, 1954. First she won the Academy Award for her performance in *Roman Holiday*, and then Broadway's Antoinette Perry Award for *Ondine*. Ironically, both times in the same week she beat out Deborah Kerr (for *From Here to Eternity* on the screen and *Tea and Sympathy* on Broadway). Receiving the Oscar from actor Jean Hersholt on the stage of Manhattan's Century Theatre following a performance of *Ondine*, she responded with brief but gracious words: "It's too much. I want to say thank you to *everybody* who, these past months and years, has helped, guided and given me so much. I'm truly, truly grateful, and terribly happy." Only three nights later came the Tony, Broadway's highest honor.

But Audrey was too modest to allow these tributes to change her. And the baroness's candid tongue

With Mel Ferrer in *Ondine*

spoke for them both when she said, "Considering that you have no talent, it's really extraordinary where you've gotten." If that sounded unnecessarily cruel, the actress interpreted the comment in an eighties interview: "She said it in the middle of the lovely successes I was having. She wasn't putting me down. She was saying how fortunate I was. Oh, I think she was right. I don't have this huge talent. I landed in this business because I had to earn a living."

Ondine appeared to affect Audrey's health, causing her anemic weight loss and emotional exhaustion. Under a doctor's care, she avoided all other commitments during the run of the play, concentrating all her energies on her work. But she never missed a performance. Actress Gaye Jordan, a charmer in her own right who understudied Hepburn and played a supporting role, recalls being in awe of her backstage—and in fear of hostile audiences, should *she* ever have to go on for the star. Luckily for her, she never did.

Before *Ondine* closed, Audrey and Mel announced engagement plans, with a ceremony planned for the near future. The baroness voiced her disapproval of her daughter's relationship with a man who was not only so much older than she, but who had been mar-

With Alan Hewitt (*left*) and Peter Brandon in *Ondine*

In *Ondine* on Broadway with Gaye Jordan, Mel Ferrer, Alan Hewitt, William Podmore, and Marian Seldes

Backstage after the *Ondine* opening on Broadway
(February 18, 1954)

still under contract to them. But, while the Hollywood company was willing to work out some kind of an "arrangement," Associated found it impossible to come up with a project suitable for her current star status.

When *Ondine* ended its sold-out run on June 26, 1954, Audrey's deteriorating health caused her doctor to recommend Switzerland and a rest cure in Gstaad. Meanwhile, Mel had a film commitment that summer in Rome in *La Madre*. Suffering from anemia as well as asthma (attributable directly to her longtime cigarette habit), she liked her new Swiss surroundings, but found the town of Gstaad intimidating with its celebrity-visibility quotient. Reporters and photographers intruded on her privacy, and curious fans made the problem even worse. Audrey found the peace and seclusion she needed in the more remote Burgenstock, near Lake Lucerne. As she recovered her health, Audrey and Mel set wedding plans for late September, to be followed by an Italian honeymoon. And so they

ried before and had children. Audrey countered by reminding her mother that *she* had wed and divorced *twice*. End of argument.

Ferrer and Hepburn loved working together in *Ondine* and hoped to interest Paramount in teaming them in a movie version, but there were problems with the Giraudoux rights protectors, who refused any changes in the text, insisting on what would amount to a filmed version of the play, parts of which would have caused problems with Production Code watchdogs. Instead, the studio held back plans to release *Sabrina* at that time and postponed it until autumn, when it was thought to have more Oscar potential, as indeed it did, bringing Audrey her second nomination. However, the statuette was awarded, the following spring, to Grace Kelly for *The Country Girl*.

There followed a dispute with Associated British, because Audrey had signed with Paramount while

Welcoming Deborah Kerr in her dressing room during the
Broadway run of *Ondine*

Still in stage makeup from *Ondine,* accepting her Academy Award for *Roman Holiday* from actor Jean Hersholt (March 25, 1954)

were wed on September 24, 1954, in Burgenstock, and spent a month in Italy. That October, the actress returned to Holland for the first time since achieving fame, in order to participate in commemorative ceremonies and receive an award for her wartime activities, which she accepted with characteristic modesty and grace. The occasion helped raise charitable donations.

The newlyweds complied with Paramount's request that they attend *Sabrina*'s successful New York and Los Angeles premieres. But before the studio could find her a new starring property, it was revealed that Audrey was pregnant, a condition that forced the Ferrers to put her fragile health first. And while Mel filmed *Oh Rosalinda!!* in London, Audrey settled into a six-room flat there. During that period, she became a virtual bone of contention between the Italian team of Carlo Ponti and Dino De Laurentiis and American producer Mike Todd, both of whom sought her for their respective film productions of Tolstoy's classic novel *War and Peace.* Ponti–De Laurentiis won out by the canny move of also hiring Mel Ferrer for one of the male leads, thus guaranteeing his adoring wife's

participation—after the birth of her baby. An agreement was worked out with Paramount by which it became equal partners with the Italians, who also had the loan of Hepburn's services. Paramount would have worldwide distribution of the picture, with British rights going to Associated British as settlement for its claims to Hepburn's contract.

With production details yet to be ironed out and six screenwriters working on the script, King Vidor was set to direct. Audrey had wanted Gregory Peck for the role of Pierre, but his unavailability led to the miscasting of Henry Fonda, amid an international company that would help ensure worldwide interest in the finished product. Since *War and Peace* would be her first appearance in a color film, its star—always self-conscious about what she considered her facial defects—was particularly concerned as to who would photograph her. She was instrumental in getting Jack Cardiff, a Briton who had won an Oscar for *Black Narcissus* and acclaim for *The Red Shoes,* among other distinguished pictures.

Following the completion of Mel's movie, the Fer-

On the Hollywood set of *Sabrina* with visitor Marlene Dietrich

rers returned to Burgenstock, a locale where Audrey wanted to settle permanently. During her confinement, she immersed herself in reading *War and Peace* and other Tolstoiana, while the production began shooting its battle scenes in Yugoslavia. Unfortunately, she suffered a miscarriage, and would likely have fallen into a serious depression had it not been for the preparation demands of relocating to Rome and the soundstages of Cinecittà for *War and Peace*. After the lightness of her recent vehicles, the dramatic demands of Tolstoy's story challenged her talents, although not so intensely as she might have anticipated from reading the book, for this was a rather cursory adaptation of a voluminous story. But what *did* tax her mightily was the strain of filming out of sequence, jumping back and forth from teenager to mature young woman. As the months of production stretched on, Mel completed his scenes and left for France to make *Eléna et les hommes* with Ingrid Bergman. It was their first marital separation, and as soon as Audrey could, she joined him in Paris.

Paramount now sought to star Audrey Hepburn in its film version of Tennessee Williams's Broadway drama *Summer and Smoke*, and she was visited by producer Hal Wallis, accompanied by the playwright himself. Following in the footsteps of the successful off-Broadway revival's Geraldine Page, as the Southern spinster who lusts for a small-town playboy-doctor, did not seem likely casting for Hepburn. And yet she seemed eager to do the picture, on the condition that Mel be cast as her leading man. Perhaps this was the factor that caused the project to be shelved until 1961, when Page was finally engaged to re-create her stage role—and won an Oscar nomination. Instead, Audrey would continue her movie career without Mel Ferrer, teaming with no less than Fred Astaire in the joyous musical *Funny Face*.

But this was not the *Funny Face* that Astaire and his sister Adele had starred in on Broadway in 1927, although rights to its title and contents had been purchased. Finally, it was decided to retain merely the title and a few of the George and Ira Gershwin songs, while adding other numbers by the composers to additional music by Roger Edens and Leonard Gershe. The actual basis for the 1957 *Funny Face* was an unproduced Gershe script called *Wedding Day*. The project began as a Paramount loan-out of Hepburn to MGM, where *Funny Face* was packaged, and where it was to have been produced, with Stanley

Between scenes of *Sabrina* with Humphrey Bogart and director Billy Wilder

Donen directing. With no Paramount films on the agenda for Hepburn, her studio finally reached an agreement with Metro by which Paramount would purchase the whole package from the other studio, and MGM would have the future services of Audrey Hepburn.

Filming on *Funny Face* began at Paramount in Hollywood, before moving to Paris, in the spring of 1956, with an eye not only to such landmarks as the Louvre and the Eiffel Tower, but also to various outdoor locations. Since the movie's plot centered on the fashion industry, Audrey insisted on the employment of a *credited* Givenchy for her wardrobe, leaving the studio's miffed Edith Head to design merely the clothes for costar Kay Thompson and the small-part actresses who played other models. After the uncredited work of Givenchy, for which Head had taken home an Oscar for *Sabrina*—an incident that had greatly upset Audrey—the actress must have savored her part in seeing justice triumph on *Funny Face*.

To get in shape for Astaire, Audrey delved into dance training with Eugene Loring, who would work with her on the film. The dance segments required her not only to partner her costar but also to do a leotard-clad solo in a beatnik nightclub. Director Donen has recalled her initial nervousness performing with Astaire, and how she kept making mistakes, until he deliberately made one himself and apologized, putting Audrey at her ease from that point on.

Fred Astaire was then fifty-seven and a veteran of twenty-eight movies, yet he took second billing to Audrey Hepburn on *Funny Face*, a tribute perhaps to the persuasive powers of Audrey's agent, Kurt Frings. However, she chose to temporarily forsake Frings's protective cloak when her friend Billy Wilder sought her for his proposed film *Ariane*. This was a sophisticated French bedroom comedy to be produced by Allied Artists, an offshoot of the old Monogram Pictures that was striving to become a Hollywood "major" through the engagement of top directors and stars. But before she could accept the role, she had to pacify both Paramount and MGM, which had yet to find an appropriate script for her loan-out deal with Paramount.

Wilder tried to get Cary Grant as Audrey's *Ariane* costar, but (unlike some of her other film partners) he considered himself too mature to play romantic scenes with a woman in her twenties—one of the reasons he had turned down the Bogart role in *Sabrina*. The solution, perhaps ill-advised, was Gary Cooper, who, despite being older than Grant, seemed unconcerned about the twenty-eight-year age gap with his leading lady. Wilder's solution to the problem was to frequently keep Cooper in the shadows, with the result that few of the movie's stills highlight Cooper, while Audrey positively glows in the prime of her youthful beauty. Some even thought that Maurice Chevalier, who portrayed her father and evinced great on-screen rapport with Audrey, would have been wise to switch roles with Gary Cooper. Before its release, *Ariane* had its title changed to the more commercial *Love in the Afternoon*.

It was during this filming that she acquired "Mr. Famous," her adored Yorkshire terrier, which was a gift from Mel, to keep her company while they were

Conferring about *War and Peace* in Rome with producer Dino De Laurentiis

Celebrating Edith Head's birthday at Paramount with Mel Ferrer

Touching up her makeup for *War and Peace*

now too mature, at twenty-eight, to re-create Colette's teenaged heroine, especially under the close scrutiny of the Metrocolor cameras. In so doing, she passed on what would become one of Metro's all-time biggest hits. A song-dubbed Leslie Caron, who had starred in the London stage edition of *Gigi*, replaced her.

The release of King Vidor's three-and-a-half-hour *War and Peace* won good reviews for Audrey but negative response for Mel Ferrer, who was once again criticized for his wooden lack of charisma. Nevertheless, the couple made plans to team anew in a lavish television production of *Mayerling* that their friend Anatole Litvak was directing for NBC's *Producers Showcase* series, which originated in New York. Litvak had turned out a classic French film of the same title in 1936, and it was hoped that he could make lightning strike again in 1957. Audrey had appeared numerous times on American television, most notably on Ed Sullivan's *Toast of the Town*, where she was twice seen in dramatic skits during the Broadway run of *Gigi*. However, several critics mistook *Mayerling* for her television debut. And although their offscreen relationship appeared as solid as ever, it must have been difficult for Ferrer to accept the fact that his famous wife was earning a handsome $150,000 for *Mayerling*, while he received merely $25,000. Despite expensive trappings and a distinguished supporting cast headed by Raymond Massey and Diana Wynyard, this drama about one of European history's most intriguing royal mysteries was not well received by the critics, though Nielsen ratings registered it as a popular event in American homes. Later on, *Mayerling* was shown in European cinemas as a "movie."

In need of a rest, Audrey now chose to reject all movie offers while she accompanied her husband to Spain and Mexico for location shooting of *The Sun Also Rises*. Among the scripts she turned down were *The Diary of Anne Frank* ("too painful" and too close to her own wartime experiences) and an adaptation of Maria von Trapp's popular memoir—two years before it became *The Sound of Music*—about evading the Nazis in World War II Austria. But Audrey *did* show interest in Kathryn Hulme's bestselling book about a Catholic missionary, *The Nun's Story*, to be adapted by playwright Robert Anderson for independent producer-director Fred Zinnemann. When Zinnemann's proposed costs approached a then-unsettling $4 million, Paramount declined to be associated

apart with their separate film assignments. The dog accompanied Audrey everywhere and was a permanent fixture on her movie sets. It also seemed to compensate for the child she had thus far been unable to have.

While filming *Love in the Afternoon* in Paris, Hepburn and Chevalier were visited by Alan Jay Lerner with an offer of starring roles in *Gigi*, the MGM musical he had written in collaboration with his partner, Frederick Loewe. But while her screen father readily accepted his proffered role, Audrey felt that she was

In Paris, rehearsing her dance steps with director Stanley Donen in preparation for
Funny Face

On the Paris set of *Love in the Afternoon,* relaxing with visitor Henry Fonda, husband Mel Ferrer, and costar Gary Cooper

with the project. Warner Brothers' Jack Warner then negotiated an offer that was accepted.

MGM, meanwhile, had yet to realize its *Funny Face* swap for Audrey Hepburn's services, which also carried a proviso that Mel Ferrer would *direct* her vehicle. For a time, *Ondine,* with Charlton Heston in Mel's old role, seemed a possibility, but the Giraudoux estate flatly rejected Metro's plans to turn their delicate fantasy into an expensive spectacle.

And yet *Ondine* wasn't that far removed from the project that Mel and Audrey finally *did* collaborate on at MGM—W. H. Hudson's literary classic, *Green Mansions.*

Audrey helped publicize *Funny Face* and *Love in the Afternoon,* both of which were released in mid-1957. But neither film was especially popular. Perhaps the former failed because it was too sophisticated for the masses (it has since gained near-cult status), and the latter, it was thought, due to a misleading publicity campaign that implied unappealing amorous activities involving its starring trio. In both films, of

course, Audrey Hepburn was cast opposite men old enough to be her father. Her continuing popularity as a movie star, it seemed, now depended increasingly on her female audiences, who copied her hairstyles, her wardrobe, and, in short, the whole Audrey Hepburn look.

While Mel Ferrer went to Germany to film *Fräulein,* Audrey remained behind in Hollywood to prepare for her demanding *Nun's Story* role. Because of her all-too-vivid war memories, she would not permit herself to set foot on German soil. And so the Ferrers, despite their customary closeness, would have to face the prospect of separations—especially with Audrey's impending African sojourn for *The Nun's Story.*

The film's "Sister Luke" was a pseudonym for Marie-Louise Habets, a Belgian woman who had renounced her vows after serving as a missionary nun for seventeen years. Casting her story for the screen offered little challenge to Fred Zinnemann; it *had* to be Audrey Hepburn. As the director wrote in his autobiography, "With the exception of Ingrid Bergman, there was at that time no star as incandescent as Audrey. She was shy, coltish, and intelligent; she looked delicate, but there was a hint of iron in the jawline that signified a stubborn will. I thought she would be ideal."

Her research for the role involved meeting at length with both Hulme and Habets, whose natural introversion melted away when she met the actress set to portray her. And so Audrey learned from the best possible source details of her attire and her behavior as a postulant that would aid verisimilitude. She was also shown operating-room procedures at a local hospital.

Exteriors for *The Nun's Story* were shot in Ghent, Belgium, and at the French convent of Froyennes, but with longer sequences in the Belgian Congo at what was then called Stanleyville (now Kisangani, Zaire). Interiors were filmed at Cinecittà in Rome.

While his wife was busy filming overseas, Ferrer took time out from planning *Green Mansions* to act in *The World, the Flesh and the Devil* for MGM. When it was completed, he took a camera crew to Colombia and Venezuela in search of exotic locations appro-

priate for *Green Mansions* backgrounds. But a reunion in Rome with Audrey, who was suffering from kidney stones, changed his mind about shooting on location, and he arranged to produce the movie in Hollywood, where he'd supervise the construction of a convincing rain forest on Metro soundstages.

The Nun's Story required the constant presence of Audrey Hepburn for a rigorous six months, and Fred Zinnemann had only praise for her work: "I have never seen anyone more disciplined, more gracious, or more dedicated to her work than Audrey. There was no ego, no asking for favors. To spare her injury, I wanted to use a stuntwoman in the scene in the lunatic asylum where she's attacked by one of the inmates (robust Colleen Dewhurst in her movie debut), but she refused. Audrey could have broken her back, but her dancer's agility helped her, and we were able to shoot the scene in one take."

Hepburn and Ferrer were reunited in Los Angeles that June. It would be nearly a year before the release of *The Nun's Story*, during which time *Green Mansions* was not only filmed but also shown to an indifferent public. The critics had scant praise for the $3 million

With director Fred Zinnemann on the set of *The Nun's Story*

Celebrating with Anthony Perkins, crew, and four-footed friend on the set of *Green Mansions*

for a long-overdue rest, during which time Audrey again found herself pregnant. Her condition overjoyed her; making *The Unforgiven*, as it turned out, did not.

The picture was filmed in Durango, Mexico, standing in for 1860s Texas, and Audrey enjoyed a good working relationship with John Huston. The director began his movie with high hopes of turning out a socially responsible drama, rather than some run-of-the-mill outdoor adventure picture. But while producer and star Burt Lancaster fought Huston's high ideals in favor of commercial success, rather than what might prove an arty "message" movie, United Artists appeared only to want plenty of red-blooded action. The result was a compromise that's not a bad picture, but one that soured Huston altogether. As he later wrote, "Everything went to hell. It was if some celestial vengeance had been loosed upon me for infidelity to my principles."

Amid production, Audrey was seriously injured when a horse she had been accustomed to riding became startled by blank-ammunition practice and threw her to the ground, fracturing four vertebrae, spraining a foot, and wrenching her lower-back muscles. Mel Ferrer wanted the film closed down and the production canceled, but the studio refused to comply, determining to shoot around its distaff star for the six

fiasco, and its utter failure smothered whatever hopes the couple might have entertained for future films together. MGM had attempted to juice up interest in the picture with deceptive advertising that promised, "Rima, the untouched, the girl of the virgin forest, meets her first man!" The man under discussion was played by Anthony Perkins, and although Audrey enjoyed their professional association, there wasn't much on-screen chemistry between them.

After these two projects, she was ready for a vacation from picture-making, but found it difficult to resist the offer for a role in a major Western—and compensation of $250,000. Produced by Hecht-Hill-Lancaster, *The Unforgiven* dealt with frontier racial prejudice, with Audrey cast as a full-blooded Kiowa Indian adopted as an infant by white Texans and raised as their own. Revelation of her true heritage is the crux of the plot. Before production got under way, the Ferrers found time to return to Burgenstock

weeks doctors predicted she'd need for recovery. With Marie-Louise Habets dutifully volunteering her services as a nurse, Audrey and Mel retreated to Los Angeles. Finally, at her own insistence, she eventually returned to Durango in a steel back brace and, although in considerable pain, proceeded to complete her role.

Returning to Switzerland at the end of shooting *The Unforgiven*, Audrey again miscarried and entered what she has termed a "black decline." But soon after the Ferrers' fifth wedding anniversary in October 1959, the couple once again celebrated a pregnancy in the household. Nervous about doing anything at all that might induce a further miscarriage, she used her condition as an excuse for refusing Alfred Hitchcock's offer to star in a Paramount adaptation of Henry Cecil's courtroom thriller, *No Bail for the Judge*. Audrey was particularly dismayed at the prospect of undergoing an attempted-rape scene. That she had already expressed interest in the project before reading the screenplay had empowered Hitchcock to secure the services of British stars Laurence Olivier and Laurence Harvey. But without Audrey Hepburn aboard, neither actor had any further interest in the film, and an angry Hitchcock turned his attention to an unpretentious little thriller called *Psycho*.

Without an Audrey Hepburn picture on its release slate since *Funny Face* in 1957, Paramount pressured her to accept one of the many scripts submitted for her approval. Among them, George Axelrod's adaptation of a Truman Capote novella called *Breakfast at*

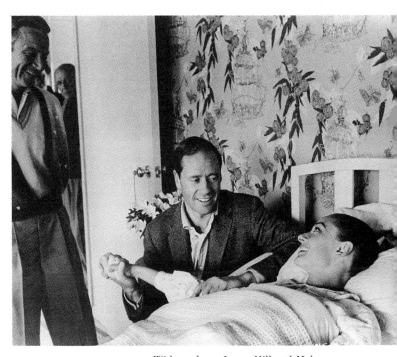

With producer James Hill and Mel Ferrer, following her injury during the location shooting of *The Unforgiven*

On the Durango, Mexico, set of *The Unforgiven*: director John Huston, Audrey, Burt Lancaster, Charles Bickford, Doug McClure, Kipp Hamilton, June Walker, Audie Murphy, and Lillian Gish

43

With Mel Ferrer at the 1959 premiere of *Ben-Hur*

Tiffany's intrigued her, although she couldn't quite see herself as a classy Manhattan kook and a playgirl who accepts money from her male escorts while dreaming of marrying a millionaire. It had originally been tailored as a vehicle for Marilyn Monroe, who was advised against playing a prostitute. Nor would Monroe's studio, Twentieth Century–Fox, consider loaning her to Paramount. Aside from any moral feelings she might have harbored about its heroine, Holly Golightly, Audrey didn't feel that she was capable of playing its flamboyant comedy scenes. But Mel urged

her to hazard the "stretch" and suggested that it might be advisable for her to consider a change of image. Director Blake Edwards and coproducer Martin Jurow even flew to Switzerland to talk her into the role, and although she maintained some reservations, she finally agreed.

Before *Breakfast at Tiffany's*, however, Audrey would avoid all work until after the birth of her child. Meanwhile, *The Nun's Story*, which had enjoyed excellent reviews and enthusiastic audiences, won her the New York Film Critics Circle award as 1959's

Visiting Mel Ferrer during the European filming of his film *Blood and Roses*

On location in New York for *Breakfast at Tiffany's* in 1960 with bespectacled director Blake Edwards and George Peppard

At the 33rd annual Academy Awards ceremony with Elizabeth Taylor and agent Kurt Frings in 1961

Best Actress, followed by her third such Academy Award nomination. For the first time, "the other Hepburn" was also among the Best Actress nominees, although both ladies lost out to Simone Signoret for *Room at the Top.* Despite its eight nominations, *The Nun's Story* failed to win any Oscars at all.

Very much in his ever popular wife's shadow, Mel Ferrer now took leading roles in insignificant, European-made coproductions, while the choice scripts were offered to Audrey. The couple continued to maintain a respected privacy concerning their personal lives, but there were the inevitable rumors that surround any show-business marriage in which the wife enjoys greater popularity—and, with it, a larger paycheck—than the husband.

On July 17, 1960, Audrey Hepburn Ferrer successfully gave birth to a healthy, nine-and-a-half-pound boy who would be named Sean, or "gift from God." At thirty-one, the new mother was naturally ecstatic and seemed more than content simply to lead a domestic life in Burgenstock. With *Breakfast at Tiffany's* on her autumn horizon, she saw no reason to consider the singing role of Hispanic Maria in the musical film of *West Side Story.* It went, instead, to Natalie Wood and a woman whose soprano voice would figure importantly in Audrey's future . . . Marni Nixon.

Breakfast at Tiffany's—which would bring Audrey

Peppard as her leading man, but found working with him difficult, due to his Method approach to acting. Her own acting technique, such as it was, simply consisted of hard work, intense concentration—and instinct. Other key roles were taken by Patricia Neal, Martin Balsam, Buddy Ebsen, and—in a blatant example of politically incorrect miscasting—Mickey Rooney, as a parody of an excitable Japanese photographer.

Givenchy whipped up some chic, high-style clothing for Audrey's endearing Holly Golightly to flaunt, and the finishing touch on a unique and delightful mix of comedy and wistful drama was the score composed by Henry Mancini. In particular, the haunting ballad "Moon River," which he wrote with lyricist Johnny Mercer, remains indelibly identified not only with *Breakfast at Tiffany's* but also with Audrey. During production, she was contacted by William Wyler, who wanted her for his remake of Lillian Hellman's *The Children's Hour*, which he had originally directed in a 1936 revision as—disguising its lesbian references—*These Three*. The story's subject matter un-

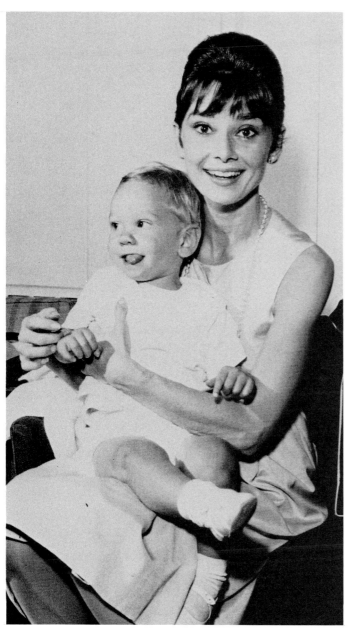

With her firstborn, three-year-old Sean Ferrer, at New York's Kennedy Airport in 1961

a fourth Oscar nomination—began production with two weeks of shooting in New York, where locations included not only that landmark Fifth Avenue store, but also a town house on East Seventy-first Street and the Women's House of Detention in Greenwich Village. The remainder was shot in Hollywood, where, photographed again by her favorite cinematographer, Franz Planer, Audrey Hepburn performed what would become one of her signature roles in what some consider her very best picture. She approved George

With "Mr. Famous" on the Hollywood set of *The Children's Hour*

47

nerved her somewhat, as did the prospect of teaming, for the first time, with another woman—especially one as talented as Shirley MacLaine. But Audrey found it difficult to refuse Wyler, who, after all, had helped her win an Oscar for *Roman Holiday*. And since her entire family was with her in Hollywood for *Breakfast at Tiffany's*, she decided to prolong her stay there.

With his 1961 version of *The Children's Hour*, Wyler hoped to be able to handle frankly Hellman's original material about two teachers falsely accused by a spiteful pupil of carrying on a lesbian relationship. But there was trepidation at United Artists about the film's content, and Shirley MacLaine, in particular, was forced to compromise her performance. For Audrey, the quiet, sober Karen Wright was a world removed from her madcap Holly Golightly, providing a welcome challenge. And despite their divergent personalities, she enjoyed unexpected on-the-set rapport with MacLaine, who has said, "Audrey and I had a running gag all through the picture. She was supposed to teach me how to dress and I was supposed to teach her how to cuss. Neither of us succeeded." James Garner, who played Hepburn's suitor in *The Children's Hour*, recalls, "It was a happy set, because of Audrey and Shirley."

In fact, the only unhappiness connected with the making of that motion picture occurred away from the studio one day when Audrey's beloved Mr. Famous got out of her house and was run over on Wilshire Boulevard. Mel quickly assuaged her grief by presenting her with a new dog, which they called Sam.

The Ferrers then returned to Europe. And while Audrey, Sean, and Sam settled back into Swiss domesticity, Mel went to France for a part in *The Longest Day*.

Breakfast at Tiffany's opened in October to record business at Radio City Music Hall and continued to do well in urban areas, but it did less well than Paramount had hoped. Its influences, however, were widespread, especially with regard to marmalade cats and female attire. At the 1961 Oscar ceremonies, held April 9, 1962, Audrey lost the statuette to Sophia Loren for *Two Women*, but she was overjoyed when Henry Mancini and Johnny Mercer won a Best Song Oscar for "Moon River"—and paid her tribute in their acceptance speech.

While the Ferrers were in Hollywood for the Academy Awards, Mel tried to set up a deal to produce a film of *Peter Pan* with Audrey in the title role (customarily played by a female) and Peter Sellers as Captain Hook. But there were insurmountable rights problems with both the James M. Barrie estate and the Disney organization.

And then came the mistake called *Paris When It Sizzles*, a Paris-made redo of the fifties French comedy *Holiday for Henrietta*, whipped together by Paramount to fulfill commitments it held with both Audrey Hepburn and her *Sabrina* teammate, William Holden. With Richard Quine directing a George Axelrod script, the prospects seemed promising for a delightful romantic farce. But the dismal result caused the studio to shelve it for two years, releasing it in the spring of 1964, after her subsequent picture, *Charade*. While filming in Paris, Hepburn and Holden were seen dining out together on more than one occasion. At the same time, on location in Madrid for *The Fall of the Roman Empire*, Ferrer was often reported in the company of a beautiful young duchess. Press and paparazzi probed and questioned, but, true to form, neither Audrey nor Mel had any comments for publication.

Charade allowed Audrey to remain on in Paris to team once more with a much older costar, Cary Grant, in a lighthearted thriller of the Hitchcock variety about a young widow, harassed by members of a sinister gang, who meets and is aided by a charming mystery man. Grant, of course, had twice rejected opportunities of romancing Audrey Hepburn on the screen, simply because he felt uneasy about their twenty-five-year age gap. But he agreed to *Charade* only because screenwriter Peter Stone consented to script changes downgrading their love scenes, while making Audrey the romantic aggressor. Stanley Donen saw no problem with the Grant-Hepburn teaming. "It was believable because Audrey had a maturity. She was vulnerable, but she had confidence. You might say that she had such self-confidence in what she was doing that she made those relationships work."

Since many of the big stars were making movie deals involving percentages, Kurt Frings arranged for *Charade* to pay Audrey her going rate of $750,000 plus a percentage of the gross. This was a fortuitous move because *Charade*, released by Universal, proved her biggest box-office hit to date. Apparently, the Grant-Hepburn combination made it impossible for audiences to resist.

Charade completed filming in February 1963, fi-

48

nally allowing the Ferrer family to regroup and settle down together and get reacquainted with one another in Switzerland. By now Audrey had been moviemaking for eight months without a vacation. And then came *My Fair Lady*, the casting for which came as the result of months of behind-the-scenes negotiations between Kurt Frings and Warner Brothers. Not only did Jack L. Warner respect Audrey's worldwide popularity, but *The Nun's Story* had been among his studio's all-time top grossers, and *My Fair Lady*—with George Cukor directing—was too costly an enterprise to take a chance on Broadway's acclaimed Julie Andrews, a virtual nobody as far as movies were concerned. For Audrey Hepburn, the role of Eliza Doolittle offered major challenges, but it was a part she very much wanted. In both *Breakfast at Tiffany's* and *Funny Face*, her pleasant, husky singing voice had been charmingly acceptable, considering the limited vocal demands of her songs. But *My Fair Lady* required a light, "legitimate" soprano, and although Audrey completed recording the soundtrack numbers, she was devastated to learn that the studio had decided to replace her songs with the voice of Marni

Gathered for the filming of *My Fair Lady*: director George Cukor, Rex Harrison, Audrey, and producer Jack L. Warner

On the *My Fair Lady* set with Rex Harrison and director George Cukor

Nixon, who had taken on similar duties for Deborah Kerr in *The King and I* and Natalie Wood in *West Side Story*. It was undoubtedly the deciding factor in the omission of her name from 1965's Best Actress Oscar nominees, although *My Fair Lady* received most favorable reviews. One who *did* get nominated,

however, was Broadway's bypassed Eliza, Julie Andrews, who won the award for her screen debut in Disney's *Mary Poppins*.

Audrey Hepburn was gracious enough to accept the Academy's invitation to step in for ailing Patricia Neal (the previous year's Best Actress) and present

49

With Rex Harrison
and Mel Ferrer at the
My Fair Lady
premiere

Presenting the Oscar to costar Rex Harrison for *My Fair Lady*

the Best Actor Oscar, which went to Audrey's *My Fair Lady* costar, Rex Harrison, reprising his stage role of Henry Higgins. Audrey was delighted, if slightly embarrassed, when Harrison held her—as well as the Oscar—throughout his acceptance speech, in which he said, "I feel in a way I should split it in half between us." The following day, Audrey sent congratulatory flowers to Julie Andrews and returned to Switzerland.

While filming *The Fall of the Roman Empire* in Madrid for producer Samuel Bronston, Mel Ferrer had suggested that Bronston consider starring Audrey Hepburn as Spain's Queen Isabella in a Cinerama-screen costume epic in which he (Mel) would be cast as Christopher Columbus—and also direct. Bronston liked the idea and even assigned screenwriter Philip Yordan to develop a script. But bankruptcy put an end to Bronston's plans. In sympathy with his career, Audrey now traveled on location with her husband, probably in an effort to keep their marriage together. Then came erroneous news that Joseph Ruston had died. Mel investigated the rumors and found that he was still alive at seventy-four and in Ireland, where the Ferrers had trouble evading reporters when they went to find him. Their reunion was bittersweet, perhaps as a result of their too-long separation. Ruston

50

appeared knowledgeable about his daughter's brilliant career but undemonstrative. "I think he was proud, but in a very Victorian sort of way," she later commented. "My mother was like that too. It was a job well done, but you didn't make a lot of fuss about it."

Warner Brothers launched *My Fair Lady* with reserved-seat engagements. The Ferrers obliged Warners by attending the picture's premieres in a succession of worldwide bookings. For Audrey it was agony, because she hadn't battled harder to avoid being dubbed. Especially humiliating was having to sit, watch, and listen while Marni Nixon's voice emanated from her throat in high-flying numbers like "I Could Have Danced All Night" and "Show Me." Not helping matters was gossip columnist Hedda Hopper's vicious snipe that "with Marni Nixon doing the singing, Audrey Hepburn gives only half a performance." Apparently, Academy voters agreed.

William Wyler, whose *The Collector* she'd previously passed on, now came back into Audrey's life, offering her the lead, opposite Peter O'Toole, in his next film—her third under his direction. This time the vehicle, *How to Steal a Million*, was a slight Harry Kurnitz script about an art forger's daughter who teams with a cat burglar to heist one of her father's phony art objects from a museum before the fraud is discovered. Filming would be completely in Paris, which had become almost a home-away-from-home for her. And, after teaming with Cary Grant and Rex Harrison, it was a pleasant change to work with a contemporary like O'Toole, who was actually three years her *junior*. Filming began in mid-1965 with Hepburn happily costumed in the designs of Givenchy, a factor that caused friction with Mel, who felt that his wife should be paid for the designer's use of her face and name in the sales of his popular fragrance, L'Interdit. Audrey believed that there was nothing wrong with helping a close friend establish his perfume business, and she resented Mel's efforts to reach a financial arrangement with Givenchy.

After the completion of the Wyler picture, the Ferrers decided it was time to set down deeper roots in Switzerland by exchanging their Burgenstock rental home for something more permanent. This they found in the quiet mountain village of Tolochenaz-sur-Morges, above Lake Geneva, where they purchased a huge and rambling old stone farmhouse, enhanced by flower gardens and protective fencing. Audrey named it La Paisible, which translates as "the peaceful place." As a getaway home for the winter months, they also bought a place on Spain's Costa del Sol, in Marbella. Audrey then found herself pregnant again, offering a perfect excuse for her to refuse any and all movie offers and confine herself to La Paisible. But a month later she miscarried, which naturally depressed her. Kurt Frings tried to interest her in one of the many scripts he sent to her. He was particularly high on MGM's idea of casting her opposite Richard Burton in a musical remake of the sentimental 1939 Oscar winner, *Goodbye, Mr. Chips*. But not even the opportunity of doing her own singing could persuade Audrey to make another musical so soon after *My Fair Lady*'s mixed blessings.

Stanley Donen offered her possible salvation with an unusual Frederic Raphael screenplay called *Two for the Road*, about the ups and downs of one couple's relationship through the years. Making it fashionably sixties was the script's intricate structure, jumping back and forth in time to tell its story in episodic fashion. Quickening Audrey's pulse were scenes of a sexual content, which concerned her. Would her fans be offended? And was she ready for a nude scene? A visit by Donen and Raphael at Tolochenaz revealed that Audrey was concerned about any radical change of her accepted screen image. Also, *Two for the Road* dealt with serious marital problems, and was for Audrey perhaps a bit too close for comfort. But she was guaranteed careful treatment and the avoidance of exploitation, and having had only favorable experiences filmmaking with Donen on *Funny Face* and *Charade*, she agreed to do the film. Albert Finney was cast as the lover who becomes her husband; the actor was seven years younger than Audrey, but this was not readily evident on the screen.

Two for the Road offered the actress her biggest "stretch" since *The Nun's Story*. Working in extraordinary rapport with both cast and production team, Audrey Hepburn gave an outstanding performance as the fun-loving Bohemian who matures into responsible womanhood, while her professionally successful husband changes little. Begun in mid-1966, *Two for the Road* employed its stars in nearly every scene, thus making it impossible for Audrey to have time for her family. With the heat of summer and the constant change of locations, Mel elected to remain in Tolochenaz with Sean, working on a deal with Kurt Frings to secure the hit Broadway thriller *Wait Until*

Dark for his wife. She, meanwhile, had discovered such close rapport with Albert Finney that rumors of an affair were rampant. Certainly, they enjoyed one another's company, shared a mischievous sense of humor, and frequently acted as though there was no one else around. Those who were used to a cool and rather withdrawn Audrey Hepburn on her sets now saw an outgoing mixer with a penchant for horseplay. As Stanley Donen has noted, "I saw an Audrey I didn't even know. She overwhelmed me. She was so free, so happy. I never saw her like that. So young! I guess it was Albie."

But *Two for the Road* eventually ended, and so did speculation about Hepburn and Finney. He returned to the stage of Britain's National Theatre, and she resumed domesticity with Mel and Sean at La Paisible.

Stanley Donen would later describe her Joanna Wallace as the best performance of Audrey's career. "The role was a departure for her. It required a depth of emotion, care, yearning, and maturity that Audrey had never played before," said the director. "She had to go very deep into herself for the part, and she did."

Oddly enough, she received no Oscar nomination for *Two for the Road*. But the Academy did accord her that honor for another 1967 release, *Wait Until Dark*, in which she played a terrorized blind woman.

Perhaps as a sign to the world that their thirteen-year union remained solid, Mel Ferrer had made it known, when filming began, that he was the producer of *Wait Until Dark*, which had starred Lee Remick on Broadway. By now Audrey Hepburn had joined Elizabeth Taylor in the $1-million-plus salary category. Jack Warner had purchased the play especially for her. *My Fair Lady* had surmounted its occasional critics to become the greatest moneymaker in Warner Brothers history, so he considered Audrey a prized property well worth showcasing in a vehicle more appropriate than musical comedy.

The Ferrers wanted Britain's Terence Young as their *Wait Until Dark* director, while Warner pressed for Carol Reed. Mel, who had also made tentative future plans with Young, got his way, and filming began in New York's Greenwich Village before shifting to California for all interiors. It wasn't an easy role for Audrey, emotionally. And at the same time, she was privately coping with the disintegration of her marriage. Her health was precarious as well; slim as she already was, she lost almost fifteen pounds while filming *Wait Until Dark*. "The role was probably the most rigorous that Audrey ever played," explained Terence Young. "She worked herself so hard that you could see the pounds rolling off her each day."

Before returning to Switzerland, Audrey welcomed a visit from Sean and her mother the baroness, whom she took on excursions to such local attractions as Disneyland and Knott's Berry Farm. She also held press interviews for *Two for the Road*, during which she promoted the myth that her home life couldn't be more serene. Privately, she and Mel argued over the future of her career: He wanted her to make more movies; she looked forward to spending more time in Tolochenaz with Sean. Unfortuitously, yet another pregnancy followed. But the familiar pattern of miscarriage transpired a month later. All during this time, Mel was back in Hollywood, supervising *Wait Until Dark*'s editing with Terence Young. The result, when it opened in November 1967 at Radio City Music Hall, was another profitable box-office winner for Warner Brothers—and the percentage-sharing Ferrers. At that time, the two were planning a return to *Mayerling*, despite their failure with the story a decade earlier. This time, Mel would produce a lavish big-screen coproduction of MGM and Gaumont Pictures, to be filmed in Austrian locations with Audrey starring opposite Omar Sharif, in her husband's former role.

But a combination of factors caused the actress to bow out: She had yet to fully emerge from the depression brought on by her latest miscarriage, and their strained working relationship on *Wait Until Dark* was still too recent and too problematic an experience for Audrey to want to chance an encore. Mel accepted her decision calmly and cast Catherine Deneuve to replace her. And while he was busy with *Mayerling*, Audrey remained at home with Sean.

That September, there came an announcement that, after thirteen years together, the Ferrers had decided to live apart. With no wish to continue working, Audrey asked Kurt Frings not to send her any more scripts or hound her with job offers. She and Sean proceeded to spend the year-end holidays in Marbella, where she was frequently reported in the company of Prince Alfonso de Bourbon-Dampierre.

Early in 1968, Audrey Hepburn won her fifth (and final) Academy Award nomination as Best Actress for *Wait Until Dark*, but that Oscar went to the *other* Hepburn, for *Guess Who's Coming to Dinner*. That

spring, Mel Ferrer settled in Los Angeles, where reports of his free-living ways discouraged Audrey from allowing Sean to visit him there. When the divorce was officially announced on November 21, 1968, details were kept private. But Audrey retained custody of eight-year-old Sean, as well as the house in Switzerland, and could still count her assets in the multimillions. From their longtime business arrangements, Ferrer emerged very wealthy indeed.

Only after a long passage of time was Audrey able to put this experience into perspective: "When my marriage to Mel broke up, it was terrible; more than that, it was a keen disappointment. I thought a marriage between two good, loving people had to last until one of them died. I can't tell you how disillusioned I was. I'd tried and tried."

Surprisingly, Audrey was the first to remarry, having been introduced to Dr. Andrea Dotti, an aristocratic Italian psychiatrist-neurologist, on a private yacht cruise of the Greek islands. She was nervous about their age difference, but not enough to curtail their romance. "Intellectually, he was older than I. His education and his work in psychiatry had matured him way beyond his years. Also, we were very close emotionally. So we met somewhere between his thirty

With Andrea Dotti on the occasion of their wedding in Morges, Switzerland, on January 18, 1969

Shopping in Rome with "Sam"

and my thirty-nine!" There was no reason for concern that Dr. Dotti would benefit from his wife's celebrity or her money. More important, there was an encouraging bonding evident between Andrea and Sean.

Because Dotti was Catholic and Audrey was a divorced Protestant, they elected to avoid contending with his church by being wed in a civil ceremony at the town hall in Morges, near her home. She would retain La Paisible as a getaway retreat, to be maintained by the Baroness van Heemstra and her staff there. Meanwhile, the newlyweds would live in Rome, where her husband had his practice, and where Sean was enrolled in a bilingual school.

Four months into her second marriage, Audrey discovered she was pregnant, an event that caused her to retreat to La Paisible to take extra precautions against her worst fears. But she need not have worried; Luca Dotti was born on February 8, 1970, in a Caesarean delivery—all the more reason now to settle into her new role as a Roman wife and mother. She seemed happy and fulfilled and philosophical about the women with whom her nightclubbing husband had been photographed during her pregnancy. "My husband and I had what you would call an open arrangement," she later admitted. "It's inevitable, when the man is younger. I wanted the marriage to last. Not just for our own sake, but for that of the son we had together."

With Andrea Dotti, railing against the ever persistent *papaparazzi*

54

With her second son, Luca Dotti, in 1970

Audrey appeared wholly content with her life in Rome, and enjoyed lunching with friends or shopping in the Via Condotti and the Via Frattina without being bothered by the public. More than cognizant of Andrea's Casanova tendencies, Audrey determined not to allow a recurrence of the situations so well reported in the tabloids during her confinement. As far as her career was concerned, it now seemed possible to consider her "retired," although she announced a willingness to act again—but only if the picture could be filmed in Rome, so as not to disrupt her family life. William Wyler expressed an interest in directing her in the romantic comedy *Forty Carats*, but Columbia Pictures ruled out filming at Rome's Cinecittà, so Wyler relinquished the job to Milton Katselas, and Liv Ullmann ill-advisedly took the role in which Audrey might have shone. She also turned down producer Sam Spiegel's offer to portray half of the title in his historical spectacle *Nicholas and Alexandra*, because she felt she was too old.

Acting now seemed utterly unimportant to Audrey. Instead of reading scripts, she preferred to learn more about Dr. Dotti's profession, and she accompanied him to lectures and on other job-related missions. She also stood up for the role of housewife: "'Keeping house' is in a very real sense just that. You have to be there to contribute. I don't want my husband and children to come home and find a rattled woman. Our era is already rattled enough, isn't it?"

Audrey divided her time between their Roman apartment and her beloved La Paisible, rarely venturing into the arena of show business. One such excursion, however, was for a 1970 Christmas television special, *A World of Love*, documenting the work of the United Nations Children's Fund (UNICEF), with her portion shot in Rome. Also produced in her adoptive home city was a series of wig commercials for a Japanese manufacturer. Audrey stipulated that they be shown only in Japan (where she remained tremendously popular), and she invested her fee of $100,000 in annuities for her sons.

Five years into their marriage, Dr. Dotti was again being seen on the town with other women. To maintain their union, Audrey resolved to keep up appearances, although confidantes knew of her unhappiness. As she told the press, "Andrea's an extrovert. I'm an introvert. He needs people and parties, while I love being by myself, love being outdoors, love taking long walks with my children and my dogs."

For one reason or another, she continued to reject movie offers, causing Luchino Visconti to replace

During the shooting of commercials for a Japanese wig manufacturer in 1971

her with Silvana Mangano in *Conversation Piece*. Nor would she accept the role French actress Jeanne Moreau had written especially for her in *Lumière*. Moreau eventually directed *herself* in that part. The one project that Audrey might have embraced—an unusual teaming with Elizabeth Taylor and, possibly, Shirley MacLaine in *Father's Day*—eventually fell through for lack of financing. But after eight years away from the screen, Audrey finally found the script and conditions conducive to a comeback—although she chose to term it simply a "return."

What finally brought her back to the world's screens was director Richard Lester's update on the Robin Hood legend, a seriocomic adventure tale of middle-aged romance, which was released as *Robin and Marian*, with Sean Connery cast in the other title role. The picture was filmed in Spain, near Pamplona, and Audrey was shocked to find that economic necessities had eliminated many of the perks she had become accustomed to in her Hollywood heyday. Nor was she used to anything less than a three-month shooting schedule. *Robin and Marian* was filmed in less than six weeks amid the extreme discomfort of a midsummer heat wave.

During her absence, Dr. Dotti's Roman nightclub rounds, usually in the company of attractive women, were duly recorded in the newspapers and were naturally a source of embarrassment to his wife. But more worrisome for Audrey, once the movie was completed, were the anonymous kidnapping threats they received targeting Sean and Luca. Their mother's recourse was to take the boys to the safer atmosphere of Switzerland. Soon afterward, Dr. Dotti was somewhat roughed up in Rome when four masked men attempted to abduct him as he was leaving a suburban clinic. His cries attracted security guards, who foiled the kidnapping. Audrey needed no further inducement to remain in Tolochenaz.

Robin and Marian was launched in the United States in spring 1976, once again at Radio City Music Hall, and Audrey flew there on a dual mission, combining her publicity junket with a personal appearance at the American Film Institute's evening honoring seventy-three-year-old William Wyler. The ceremony, which was later telecast on CBS, had Audrey introducing film clips and presenting AFI scholarship awards to deserving students. In her personal tribute, she said, "If it weren't for Willy Wyler, I wouldn't have learned how to act."

Dr. Dotti flew over from Rome to join her for the Academy Awards ceremony, at which Audrey, in a pink Givenchy gown, presented the Best Picture Oscar to producer Michael Douglas for *One Flew Over the Cuckoo's Nest*. Her very appearance, after so many years away from the Hollywood spotlight, brought her a standing ovation from her peers.

Appearing more mature at forty-six than when last the public had seen her eight and a half years earlier in *Wait Until Dark*, Audrey was gratefully welcomed back by fans and critics alike. But reviews for *Robin and Marian* were mixed, and after an initial flurry of box-office interest, attendance dwindled. Quite likely, younger moviegoers—always the bulk of a cinema audience—found little to identify with in a story centering on middle-aged characters.

Robin and Marian brought Audrey Hepburn some film offers, but none that she chose to accept, including producer Joseph E. Levine's all-star adaptation of the Cornelius Ryan bestseller *A Bridge Too Far*, in which she would have played a Dutch mother who aids the wounded Allies in Holland during World War II. Not wishing to relive unpleasant memories, she relinquished the role to Liv Ullmann. The Norwegian actress, who had replaced her in *Forty Carats*, continued to do so in the obscure lesbian drama *Richard's Things*. Too late, Audrey found out about an exciting script called *The Turning Point*, but her longtime agent Kurt Frings had no luck trying to persuade director Herbert Ross to replace Anne Bancroft with his client. Another project Audrey turned down was the dramatic NBC miniseries *The Best Place to Be*, which Donna Reed accepted.

With her husband's need to be in Rome for his work—and where the other women of his acquaintance now appeared to be ever younger—Audrey realized the widening gap that separated her from Andrea, not only in age but certainly in lifestyles. In one tabloid, an unnamed Dotti friend was quoted: "It's unfortunate that the paparazzi hound Andrea. But it's also unfortunate that he gives them the opportunity. They wouldn't be able to snap those awful pictures if he was more discreet or stopped chasing, but that's as unlikely as his giving up pasta or risotto."

Characteristically, Audrey tried to protect her marriage by insisting that they had their differences, like any couple, but that they were "basically happy." But more than three years after the completion of *Robin and Marian*, she was so desperate for distraction that she agreed to star—for a million plus a percentage—in a Sidney Sheldon thriller called *Bloodline*. Her name enabled this international coproduction to line up distinguished actors like James Mason, Irene Papas, and Omar Sharif to populate a movie about a young cosmetics heiress caught up in a tawdry story of sex and violence. *Wait Until Dark*'s Terence Young directed unremarkably and may have neglected to inform Audrey that the role had already been turned down by Candice Bergen, Diane Keaton, and Jacqueline Bisset—any of whom would have been better suited, agewise.

Audrey's romantic vis-à-vis in *Sidney Sheldon's Bloodline*, as it was egotistically retitled before release, was Ben Gazzara, who was then separated from his actress-wife Janice Rule. His on-and-off-the-set rapport with Audrey led to considerable press speculation about an affair. But the movie finished shooting, and she returned to her husband in Italy. Then, to help save their union, she engineered a second-honeymoon trip to the Far East. The result was no solution; the Dottis now quarreled more often than not. Were it not for ten-year-old Luca, who adored both his parents, a divorce would have been the immediate answer.

With director Richard Lester during the filming of *Robin and Marian* in Spain (1975)

The release of *Sidney Sheldon's Bloodline* brought only disastrous notices for the film, although many of the critics were obviously too devoted to Audrey Hepburn to be anything but kind and commiserating. The experience caused her to consider actual and permanent retirement, for she didn't need the money and she harbored no wish to finish off her career in the cheap thrillers that had embarrassingly completed the filmographies of some of the movies' once-great female stars.

For some reason, she liked writer-director Peter Bogdanovich and his script for a quirky comedy called *They All Laughed*, and she accepted a smallish role—but with top billing—in this Manhattan-filmed little picture. Perhaps the recurring presence of Ben Gazzara, once again performing opposite her, was the inducement. Whatever the case, Audrey's promised cooperation ensured financing of an iffy project. And Sean Ferrer, who had already worked at various behind-the-scenes jobs on Terence Young's *Inchon*, was hired to double as production assistant and play a small acting role as well.

Meanwhile, the press scented a Hepburn-Gazzara romance, which the actor attempted to deflect with platitudinous comments about his admiration of her as a professional. It has been reported that when he felt their resumed relationship was growing too serious for comfort, Gazzara deliberately flaunted his younger

With Sean Connery at the New York premiere of *Robin and Marian* (1976)

With son Sean Ferrer at the American Film Institute Salute to Fred Astaire (1980)

Andrea's marriage to Audrey Hepburn was officially ended.

Audrey had already met the man who would bring her love and companionship in her final years. His name was Robert Wolders, and he had been born in the Netherlands seven years her junior. A former actor, he had met and married wealthy actress Merle Oberon when she was fifty-five and he only thirty-four. They had enjoyed nine years together before her death in 1979.

Rob Wolders and Audrey realized a great deal in common, from mutual interests to similar European backgrounds. As he later recalled, "We liked each other immediately. It was a normal, friendly kind of contact we had, nothing more. I liked her a lot, and she really did try to put me at ease. Audrey had known Merle and admired her. She understood her death was a great loss to me, and encouraged me to talk about it."

News of her father's serious illness brought the two closer together when Wolders offered to accompany

lady-friends on the set, causing his professional relationship with Audrey to end on a chilly note. *They All Laughed* would mark Audrey Hepburn's last starring role in a theatrical motion picture.

One concept that might have worked was Kurt Frings's notion of reuniting his client with Gregory Peck in a *Roman Holiday* sequel. But there were legal constraints on the original material. In an interview, Audrey allowed that she'd welcome an opportunity to play older character parts, but none seemed to be forthcoming. Perhaps no one in the industry was ready to embrace the notion of an aging Audrey Hepburn.

In September of 1980, the news that everyone had long anticipated was made public when Dr. Dotti's stepfather, Vero Roberti, announced to the press that

With constant companion Robert Wolders at the London Film Festival in 1986

58

her on the emotionally difficult trip to Dublin for her final visit with the ninety-year-old Joseph Ruston. Since their 1964 reunion, she had quietly extended him financial aid, although her affection had brought no tangible reciprocation. Three days after their arrival, he died. News of his funeral and burial was somehow kept from the press.

Because she was still legally wed, Audrey maintained care in her growing relationship with Rob Wolders, for fear of custodial repercussions regarding Luca, for whom his father wanted a traditional Italian upbringing. But Wolders eventually moved in with her at La Paisible, and friends noted a happier, more content Audrey Hepburn. Her one problem now seemed to be Luca's aversion to the new man in her life. Audrey also had the care of her elderly mother, who had become a frail invalid while living with her in Tolochenaz.

In 1982, the Dotti divorce was finalized, but Audrey made no move to legalize her relationship with Rob Wolders, the relaxed social attitudes of the eighties having ascribed no particular stigma to their living arrangements. Wolders accompanied her to Los Angeles for an American Film Institute tribute to Fred Astaire, as well as to other parts of the world on other missions.

On August 26, 1984, the Baroness Ella van Heemstra died at Le Paisible at the age of eighty-four. It left Audrey bereft: "I was lost without my mother. She had been my sounding board, my conscience. She was not the most affectionate person—in fact there were times when I thought she was cold—but she loved me in her heart, and I knew that all along. I never got that feeling from my father, unfortunately."

Audrey Hepburn had now been inactive in her profession for four years. For a time, it seemed that a costly nonsinging version of *The Merry Widow* might bring her together with either director Ingmar Bergman or Franco Zeffirelli. But again, the obstacle of interesting audiences in a middle-aged romance seemed unlikely to earn back the costs of a lavish costume film, especially now that Audrey was in her mid-fifties.

Sean Ferrer, who worked in Los Angeles as a junior executive in television and motion-picture production, made Audrey a mother-in-law in 1985 when he married Marina Spadafora, the daughter of an international fashion manufacturer. It was not a union that would endure. Audrey attended the ceremony with

As Goodwill Ambassador to UNICEF, Audrey holds a child in Ethiopia in 1988. This John Isaac photo was Audrey's favorite photo of herself.

Wolders, while Mel Ferrer was also present in the company of Lisa, his wife of fourteen years. As parents of the groom, Audrey and Mel danced together for the first time in seventeen years.

In 1986, Audrey Hepburn was among a group of notables interviewed for inclusion in *Directed by William Wyler*, a well-received documentary tribute to the great filmmaker, produced by his daughter Catherine.

59

A year later, Audrey allowed Kurt Frings to talk her into doing a television movie opposite Robert Wagner. Television had become a medium popular with older, waning stars who could no longer attract audiences to theatrical screens. With no need for the added income, Audrey may have accepted this offer to help out her now elderly agent, thus enabling him to realize his 10 percent of her $750,000 salary. *Love Among Thieves*, as the feature was eventually called, was little more than a poor man's *Charade* that attracted impressive audience ratings but mostly negative reviews in the autumn of 1987. It was Audrey's last starring role.

A few weeks after completing that telefeature, Audrey was officially appointed to succeed Danny Kaye, who died in March 1987, as Goodwill Ambassador for UNICEF, an organization she'd previously helped out at fund-raising special events. Without a busy career to pursue, and with both of her sons living away from her home (Luca was now with his father in Rome), she visualized a means not only of doing something useful with her time but also of repaying the United Nations for rescuing her from starvation in 1945 Holland. "It's that wonderful old-fashioned idea that others come first and you come second," she said, explaining her motivations. "This was the whole ethic by which I was brought up. Others matter more than you do, so 'don't fuss, dear; get on with it.'"

Accompanied by Rob Wolders, she visited the young victims of war and drought in such locales as Ethiopia, the Sudan, El Salvador, Bangladesh, and Vietnam. Forcing herself to put aside her natural shyness for the sake of her mission, Audrey spoke to the press at news conferences and allowed herself to be photographed with starving children, because she knew it would attract world attention to her cause. As she later reflected, "I'm glad I've got a name, because I'm using it for what it's worth. It's like a bonus that my career has given me."

When she wasn't visiting the afflicted, she helped raise funds for UNICEF. In this respect, Audrey managed to overcome her previous aversion to the press, and she granted television and newspaper interviews. The once formidable prospect of being interviewed by Barbara Walters was now permissible, since it enabled Audrey to talk about UNICEF.

Much of her work was very hard, especially the experiences in third-world countries, where situations were frequently dangerous as well as rugged. Upon her return, Audrey would describe these experiences with the emotional honesty and compassion that captured public attention. Now, instead of stylish haute couture designed by Givenchy, Audrey was more often seen in simple khaki, T-shirts, and turtlenecks, although she still wore the occasional Givenchy gown at gala functions. In Wolders, she found an understanding soulmate, explaining, "I could never have worked for UNICEF without Robbie. Apart from my personal feelings, there's just no way I could do the job by myself."

In 1989, Audrey Hepburn turned sixty, and she agreed to be photographed for Revlon's ongoing "What Becomes a Legend Most?" ad campaign. She also accepted a cameo role in Steven Spielberg's *Always*, a lukewarm remake of the 1943 MGM fantasy *A Guy Named Joe*, in which she played a sort of heavenly messenger opposite Richard Dreyfuss.

In 1991, she hosted a PBS special called *The Fred Astaire Songbook*, as well as the eight-part syndicated television series, *Gardens of the World*, in which she visited landscaped locales in the United States, Great Britain, France, Holland, Italy, the Dominican Republic, and Japan. When this project also became the subject of a book, with part of the proceeds going to UNICEF, Audrey made a personal appearance to sign copies at the Manhattan store of her designer friend Ralph Lauren. The crowd she attracted was so large that not everyone could be accommodated.

Audrey also agreed, if somewhat reluctantly, to retrospective tributes to her career from such organizations as New York's Film Society of Lincoln Center and the U.S.A. Film Festival in Dallas—as long as UNICEF might benefit from such occasions.

As an alternate means of fund-raising for UNICEF, she collaborated with composer-conductor Michael Tilson Thomas on a series of concerts they called *Concerts for Life*, which consisted of music by Mozart and Prokofiev and featured Audrey reading from the diaries of Anne Frank. "It's a privilege to speak her words," said Audrey. "Also, it's a privilege to speak for all the children who cannot speak for themselves. Anne Frank and I were the same age, you know."

In March of 1992, Audrey made her final appearance on an Academy Awards telecast to present an honorary Oscar to India's great filmmaker Satyajit Ray, who was too ill to attend. And she was a participant in the television special *Danny Kaye's International Children's Awards*, which was taped in the

Netherlands but did not air until May 1993.

In the summer of 1992, Audrey Hepburn began to suffer abdominal discomforts, which she dismissively attributed to having put up with the poor living conditions prevalent in her third-world travels. Her Swiss doctors recommended hospital tests, but Audrey had no wish to postpone her planned UNICEF tour of Somalia. By now, her appearance caused some concern for her well-being. As a local United Nations official in Somalia said, "We pleaded with her to rest and not push herself too hard, but she refused. She insisted on taking a grueling twenty-four-hour trip by Land-Rover to a refugee camp at Baydhabo, where hundreds of children had died."

Throughout the African trip, Audrey's intestinal pains persisted. Her doctors suspected an amoebic infection, but at the insistence of friends and family in Switzerland, she consented to fly to Los Angeles for testing at Cedars-Sinai Medical Center, an institution known for protecting the privacy of celebrity patients.

Three days later, on November 2, 1992, she was operated on for colon cancer. A hospital spokesman informed the press, "There is a strong feeling that surgeons removed all of the malignancy and that none of her organs was compromised." But tabloid newspa-

Being interviewed by Prof. Richard Brown for his AMC series, *Reflections on the Silver Screen*, in 1990

per stories began to suggest otherwise. The *National Enquirer* claimed that Audrey Hepburn had been given only three months to live.

Both of her sons joined Rob Wolders at Audrey's bedside while she recovered from surgery at the Beverly Hills home of her close friend Connie Wald. But she wanted to spend Christmas back at La Paisible in Tolochenaz, and friends arranged for a private jet to take her back to Switzerland. Although her loved ones knew that the end was near for her, they continued to guard her privacy and fend off press inquiries. With nurses in attendance, Audrey was occasionally strong enough for short but invigorating walks in her beloved garden.

Cheering her final weeks, news came from Washington, D.C., that she was to receive the Presidential Medal of Freedom for 1992 because of her work for UNICEF. It was delivered to her in person by the U.S. ambassador to Switzerland.

In December, before leaving Los Angeles, she had been informed by the Screen Actors Guild that she would be the recipient in January of the SAG Achievement Award. Delighted, she responded that she would attend and accept that tribute in person. Perhaps aware that she would be unable to fulfill that commitment Audrey composed an acceptance speech, which was read for her by Julia Roberts at the ceremony on January 10, 1993. In part, it said:

> I am more than ever awed and overwhelmed
> by the monumental talents it was my great, great

As host for the 1991 TV special *The Fred Astaire Songbook*

61

privilege to work for and with. There is therefore no way I can thank you for this beautiful award without thanking all of them, because it is they who helped and honed, triggered and taught, pushed and pulled, dressed and photographed—and with endless patience and kindness and gentleness, guided and nurtured a totally unknown, insecure, inexperienced, skinny broad into a marketable commodity.

I am proud to have been in a business that gives pleasure, creates beauty, and awakens our conscience, arouses compassion, and perhaps most importantly, gives millions a respite from our so violent world.

Thank you, Screen Actors Guild and friends, for this huge honor—and for giving me this unique opportunity to express my deepest gratitude and love to all those who have given me a career that has brought me nothing but happiness.

This was Audrey Hepburn's last public statement. The award and a videotape of the ceremony were sent to Tolochenaz, where she received them two weeks before her death.

At the start of 1993, the Academy of Motion Picture Arts and Sciences announced that both Audrey Hepburn and Elizabeth Taylor would be given the Jean Hersholt Humanitarian Award, to honor their public service, at the March Oscars ceremony.

Less than four months before her sixty-fourth birthday, Audrey died quietly in her sleep on January 20, 1993. Her passing was disclosed to the media by UNICEF director James Grant, who said, "Children everywhere will feel her death as a painful and irreplaceable loss."

Amid the flood of tributes aired and published about Audrey Hepburn, Elizabeth Taylor's eloquent words would be the most quoted: "Audrey was a lady with an elegance and a charm that was unsurpassed, except by her love for underprivileged children all over the world. God has a most beautiful new angel now that will know just what to do in heaven."

Among the many flowery tributes, one of the sweetest and simplest was that placed by Tiffany's in the *New York Times*, which read:

> A U D R E Y H E P B U R N
> 1929–1993
> *Our Huckleberry Friend*
> *T I F F A N Y & C O.*

Audrey was buried in the cemetery at Tolochenaz-sur-Morges on January 24, 1993. Among those present at the funeral service, in addition to her two sons and Rob Wolders, were her brother Ian Quarles von Ufford, Dr. Andrea Dotti, Hubert de Givenchy, executives of UNICEF, actor friends Alain Delon and Roger Moore, and a noticeably saddened Mel Ferrer. Presiding over the simple service was eighty-three-year-old Maurice Eindiguer, the retired pastor who had married Hepburn and Ferrer thirty-nine years earlier. He said, "She was an angel in the Biblical sense. Even in her illness, she visited those children of Somalia, and in their faces was a light reflected from her smile."

Sean Ferrer was the last to speak, concluding, "She believed in one thing above all. She believed in love. She believed love could heal, fix, mend, and make everything fine and good in the end. And it did. She left us with peace, serenity, and her passage was almost devoid of any pain."

In the *Hollywood Reporter*, columnist Robert Osborne remembered Audrey: "The way she classed up

Hollywood's image was incalculable, although she always discounted her own importance as a star. Lest anyone has ever been cynical enough to question it, that selflessness she displayed for UNICEF was absolutely genuine. She'd never agree, but it was work she really shouldn't have been doing. Of all people, Audrey Hepburn was not a person who could see bloated babies and ever forget it; she could not look into the eyes of suffering people and ever sleep peacefully again. She was a brilliant, irreplaceable image for UNICEF, but that affiliation mightily took its toll on her."

An adoring documentary called *Audrey Hepburn Remembered* premiered on PBS-TV stations in midsummer 1993. Produced by Gene Feldman and Suzette Winter, it was a well-edited but all-too-brief blend of film clips and interviews that only served to whet the appetite for revisiting the major Hepburn movies in their entirety.

In the autumn of 1994, *People* magazine reported that "fledgling film producer" Sean Ferrer and his second wife, Leila, had forsaken Los Angeles to live at La Paisible with their baby, while twenty-four-year-old Luca Dotti now made his home in Paris, where he had become a graphic artist. Rob Wolders, it added, had moved to Rochester, New York, to be near his elderly mother. These three had recently set up in her honor the Audrey Hepburn Hollywood for Children Fund to raise money for various worldwide children's charities. Chaired by Sean, the foundation had already secured for its advisory board Julia Roberts, Winona Ryder, and Whoopi Goldberg. Among their first acts was connecting up with a fund-raiser centered on the restoration of *My Fair Lady*.

In young Luca's words, "We *had* to do this. Not only because it's good, but also because we had a responsibility to my mother."

And Rob Wolders adds, "Audrey always felt that if she inspired her own children to continue her work, that would be her greatest reward."

Walking through painter Claude Monet's famed gardens at Giverny, France, during the filming of the TV series *Gardens of the World*

With Rex Harrison and Wilfrid Hyde-White in *My Fair Lady*

THE FILMS

NEDERLANDS IN ZEVEN LESSEN   As the KLM air hostess

Nederlands in Zeven Lessen

(DUTCH IN SEVEN LESSONS/DUTCH ON THE DOUBLE)

CAST

Wam Heskes (*The Cameraman/Narrator*); Audrey Hepburn (*KLM Stewardess*); Han Bents van den Berg; Koos Koon.

CREDITS

Director-Writer: Charles Huguenot van der Linden; *Producer*: Hein Josephson; *Running time*: 39 minutes.

ORIGINAL RELEASE

1948; a DUTCH INDEPENDENT RELEASE.

THE FILM

Nearly a half century after its completion, this Dutch production is chiefly known as the film that marked Audrey Hepburn's debut in a professional motion picture. Descriptions of the movie have ranged from "a second-feature comedy" to "a travelogue of the Netherlands," with records of its length varying from thirty-nine to seventy-nine minutes. Reportedly, the former is correct, which makes it what is best known in the trade as a "featurette," designed to supplement the main attraction in cinemas of its late-forties era.

NEDERLANDS IN ZEVEN LESSEN

Today, any such production would most likely be shown, if at all, on television.

Originally, this was to have been a travel short on the Netherlands, financed by England's J. Arthur Rank. But at a time when Rank's fortunes were in a bad way, funding fell short and agreements with its

Dutch filmmakers were broken. Thus, Hein Josephson and Charles van der Linden were left with thousands of feet of film of the Netherlands, photographed from the air. This they cleverly managed to recycle by devising a film-within-the-film scenario involving a cameraman who's given a week to photograph the aerial highlights of Holland for a travelogue. Aside from Wam Heskes, the actor cast as the photographer, the remainder of the cast were nonprofessionals, including Audrey Hepburn, in the bit role of a KLM stewardess. Her screen test for the picture, photographed outdoors in her best dress, was even incorporated into the film, along with a scene in which she ushers Wam Heskes to his plane.

At eighteen, Audrey Hepburn was thrilled to be acting in a motion picture, and to be paid fifty guilders for doing so. Understandably, Charles van der Linden would proudly claim that it was *he*, not the British or Hollywood filmmakers, who had actually "discovered" Audrey Hepburn!

One Wild Oat

ONE WILD OAT

CAST

Robertson Hare (*Humphrey Proudfoot*); Stanley Holloway (*Alfred Gilbey*); Sam Costa (*Mr. Pepys*); Andrew Crawford (*Fred Gilbey*); Vera Pearce (*Mrs. Gilbey*); June Sylvaine (*Cherrie Proudfoot*); Robert Moreton (*Throstle*); Constance Lorne (*Mrs. Proudfoot*); Gwen Cherrill (*Audrey Cuttle No. 1*); Irene Handl (*Audrey Cuttle No. 2*); Ingeborg Wells (*Gloria Samson*); Charles Groves (*Charles*); Joan Rice (*Annie*); and (in unidentified bit roles) Audrey Hepburn, Fred Berger, and William (later "James") Fox.

CREDITS

Director: Charles Saunders; *Producer*: John Croydon; *Screenwriters*: Vernon Sylvaine and Lawrence Huntington; *Based on the play by* Vernon Sylvaine; *Cinematographer*: Robert Navarro; *Editor*; Marjorie Saunders; *Music*: Stanley Black; *Running time*: 78 minutes.

ORIGINAL RELEASE

1951; an Eros release of a Coronet Films production.

THE FILM

Audrey Hepburn made an inauspicious British screen debut in this now-obscure little farce, based on Vernon Sylvaine's stage success of a season earlier. Lightweight and typically English, it provided an amusing vehicle for popular comedians Robertson Hare and Stanley Holloway (destined to play Audrey's father thirteen years later in *My Fair Lady*). The men portray longtime enemies, whose offspring fall in love and resolve to end the old feud by marrying, a notion which doesn't sit well with either father. Solicitor Hare tries to prevent the union by digging up embarrassing aspects of young Andrew Crawford's past. Instead, he unearths scandal involving the philandering Holloway, thus pushing the latter to reciprocate in kind.

Hepburn's small role, as a hotel receptionist unwittingly caught up in Hare's smarmy scheme to discredit Holloway, became even briefer when the British censors deemed those scenes too risqué. As a result, editing reduced Audrey's part to two fleeting appearances to become just another pretty new face. In the early fifties, "adult" material that got by in the theater sometimes failed to meet the more restrictive standards of the cinema.

Nor did *One Wild Oat*, with its little-known (outside of the United Kingdom) cast, appeal to American distributors. And, unlike others of her early films, this one didn't show enough of Audrey Hepburn to make even a delayed import feasible, once she had become an international star in *Roman Holiday* in 1953.

CRITICS' CIRCLE

"*One Wild Oat* has been transferred to the screen with the minimum of adjustment. It is given the broad laughter treatment that rates high with British audiences, but it cannot expect to make anything of an impact on the U.S. market. It's clearly a product for home consumption, and not for export."

—"Myro.," *Variety*

"Modest film version of a popular West End farce."

—*Halliwell's Film Guide*

"Competently routine adaptation of a hit stage farce; a little dated."

—David Quinlan, *British Sound Films*

ONE WILD OAT   Robertson Hare and Stanley Holloway

70

Laughter in Paradise

CAST

Alastair Sim (*Deniston Russell*); Fay Compton (*Agnes Russell*); Beatrice Campbell (*Lucille Grayson*); Veronica Hurst (*Joan Webb*); Guy Middleton (*Simon Russell*); George Cole (*Herbert Russell*); A. E. Matthews (*Sir Charles Robson*); Joyce Grenfell (*Elizabeth Robson*); Anthony Steel (*Roger Godfrey*); John Laurie (*Gordon Webb*); Eleanor Summerfield (*Sheila Wilcott*); Ronald Adam (*Mr. Wagstaffe*); Leslie Dwyer (*Sergeant*); Ernest Thesiger (*Endicott*); Hugh Griffith (*Henry Russell*); Michael Pertwee (*Stuart*); Audrey Hepburn (*Cigarette Girl*); Mackenzie Ward (*Benson*); Charlotte Mitchell (*Ethel*).

CREDITS

Producer-Director: Mario Zampi; *Screenwriters*: Michael Pertwee and Jack Davies; *Cinematographer*: William McLeon; *Editor*: Giulio Zampi; *Art Director*: Ivan King; *Music*: Stanley Black; *Running time*: 93 minutes.

ORIGINAL RELEASE

1951; an associated British-Pathé Pictures release of a Transocean film. *U.S. Distributor*: Stratford Pictures.

THE FILM

Audrey Hepburn's second appearance under contract to Associated British gave her equally little to do—as a nightclub's cigarette girl—but at least the picture was a bit more prestigious. And its distributor even released still photographs featuring Audrey with Guy Middleton, one of the movie's top-billed stars.

In Britain, *Laughter in Paradise* was among 1951's top moneymakers. Its intriguing plot hinges on the eccentric idea of a wicked practical joker who dies and leaves his four heirs a £50,000 fortune on the condition that each fulfills an unlawful or humiliating requirement, as specified in the will. Thus, his snobbish spinster sister (Fay Compton) must spend a month in domestic employment; a hack-mystery-writer cousin will commit a petty crime, punishable by a brief term in jail; a man-about-town (Guy Middleton) has to marry the next single woman he encounters; and a timid clerk (George Cole) must pretend to hold up his bank manager.

Only a month after the release of *One Wild Oat*, a small-part player was now accorded "introducing Audrey Hepburn" billing in *Laughter in Paradise*. Some sources erroneously list this as the actress's film debut.

A 1970 British remake was entitled *Some Will, Some Won't.*

CRITICS' CIRCLE

"Producer-director Mario Zampi nearly succeeds in bringing off an outstanding comedy with *Laughter in Paradise.* Although it is not 100 percent as a nonstop laughter-maker, it rates very high as a box office attraction and should do substantial gross in the home market. Film also has distinct potentialities for American distributors who are in search of original escapist offerings."

—"Myro.," *Variety*

"It is, at best, an extended antic that only occasionally is inventive. Despite a truly surprising ending, *Laughter in Paradise* is merely pleasant, not especially surprising, comedy."

—A. H. Weiler, *New York Times*

"The whole adds up to a modest little time-killer."

—Jesse Zunser, *Cue*

"Audiences love this 1951 English comedy, and for good reason. Alastair Sim has a classic comic sequence (trying to get arrested) and a classic fiancée (Joyce Grenfell, a WAAF whom he describes as "an officer and a gentleman"). Mario Zampi's direction is not all it should be, but the cast is so good it hardly matters."

—Pauline Kael, *Kiss Kiss Bang Bang*

"A funny idea gets halfhearted treatment, but the good bits are hilarious."

—Halliwell's *Film Guide*

LAUGHTER IN PARADISE   With Guy Middleton

YOUNG WIVES' TALE   With Guy Middleton, Nigel Patrick, Joan Greenwood, Derek Farr, and Helen Cherry

Young Wives' Tale

CAST

Joan Greenwood (*Sabina Pennant*); Nigel Patrick (*Rodney Pennant*); Derek Farr (*Bruce Banning*); Guy Middleton (*Victor Manifold*); Athene Seyler (*Nanny Gallop*); Helen Cherry (*Mary Banning*); Audrey Hepburn (*Eve Lester*); Fabia Drake (*Nurse Blott*); Irene Handl and Joan Sanderson (*Nurses at Regents Park*); Selma Vaz Dias (*Ayah*); Anthony Deaner (*Valentine*); Carol James (*Elizabeth*); Jack McNaughton (*Taxi Driver*); Brian Oulton (*Man in Pub*).

CREDITS

Director: Henry Cass; *Producer*: Victor Skutezky; *Screenwriter*: Ann Burnaby; *Based on the play by* Ronald Jeans; *Cinematographer*: Erwin Hillier; *Editor*: E. Jarvis; *Art Director*: Terence Verity; *Assistant Director*: Jack Martin; *Music*: Philip Green; *Running time*: 79 minutes. Available on videocassette.

ORIGINAL RELEASE

1951; an Associated British-Pathé Picture. *U.S. Distributors*: Stratford Pictures (1952) and Allied Artists (1954).

THE FILM

A 1950s British-style situation comedy, *Young Wives' Tale* now seems very old-fashioned and trivial, and can best be enjoyed on video for the unique comedy technique of the irreplaceable Joan Greenwood—and, of course, for a longer look at the early Audrey Hepburn than permitted by her previous film appearances. As a tall, slim, and pretty but featherbrained young bachelor girl, she is attractive and well-groomed. But that now-familiar Hepburn charisma has yet to surface, and her quiet charm has its limits. The acting novice hasn't yet learned enough about moviemaking to enchant us with her smile, and the camera continues searching for a key to record her magic.

London's wartime housing shortage puts two divergent married couples, the Pennants (Joan Greenwood and Nigel Patrick) and the Bannings (Helen Cherry and Derek Farr), and their infant offspring into the same town house, which they share with a prim, unmarried lodger named Eve (Hepburn). The predictable humor derives from a madcap succession of mishaps and misunderstandings, mostly surrounding their problems in getting or retaining a nanny for the infants. Finally, they appear to have landed the per-

73

fect nursemaid in Nanny Gallop (the wonderful Athene Seyler)—only to lose her when a misunderstood familiarity between one wife and another husband is taken for immoral behavior.

The seventh-billed Hepburn's peripheral, in-and-out role introduces a minor subplot involving her neurosis about being followed in the street by predatory males. But it's amusing, on this occasion, to witness an intelligent performer's natural sensibilities supplanted by those of a skittish birdbrain.

Young Wives' Tale enjoyed but a brief U.S. release by Stratford Pictures in late 1952. To cash in on *Roman Holiday*, Allied Artists rereleased it, publicizing Audrey Hepburn, in 1954.

CRITICS' CIRCLE

"A playwright and his slaphappy wife share a house with a super-efficient couple. Very mild but palatable comedy."

—*Halliwell's Film Guide*

"More than the British housing situation looks bad in the British picture *Young Wives' Tale*, which put in a cheerless appearance at the Paris yesterday; the quality of British comedy writing seems to have dropped to an alarming degree. For what we have in this picture, which might courteously be termed a comedy, is as dismal a domestic situation as ever leaked from an uninspired brain.

To say that this nonsense is witless and foolish is putting it mildly. And no matter how hard Joan Greenwood, Nigel Patrick, Derek Farr and others try—including that pretty Audrey Hepburn as the unwed boarder—it stays on the ground."

—Bosley Crowther, *New York Times*

"*Tale* was made a number of years back by Victor Skutezky for Associated British, with Henry Cass directing a script written by Ann Burnaby. Miss Hepburn was then an unknown. She appears in this in only seven scenes, mostly inconsequential. Performances are as freewheeling as the broad plotting. Miss Greenwood . . . seems expert at the British-flavored humor, as do Patrick, Farr, Miss Cherry, Athene Seyler, Bruce [sic] Middleton and Miss Hepburn."

—"Brog.," *Variety* (reviewed from Hollywood upon the occasion of its 1954 American rerelease)

YOUNG WIVES' TALE   With Joan Greenwood and Nigel Patrick

THE LAVENDER HILL MOB On the
set with Alec Guinness

The Lavender Hill Mob

CAST
Alec Guinness (*Henry Holland*); Stanley Holloway (*Pendlebury*); Sidney James (*Lackery*); Alfie Bass (*Shorty*); Marjorie Fielding (*Mrs. Chalk*); John Gregson (*Farrow*); Edie Martin (*Miss Evesham*); Clive Morton (*Station Sergeant*); Ronald Adam (*Turner*); Sydney Tafler (*Clayton*); Jacques Brunius (*Official*); Meredith Edwards (*P. C. Edwards*); Gibb McLaughlin (*Godwin*); Patrick Barr (*Inspector*); Marie Burke (*Señora Gallardo*); Audrey Hepburn (*Chiquita*); John Salew (*Parkin*); Arthur Hambling (*Wallis*); Frederick Piper (*Cafe Proprietor*); Peter Bull (*Joe the Gab*); Patric Doonan (*Craggs*); Alanna Boyce (*Schoolgirl With Paperweight*); and (in unidentified bit roles) William (later "James") Fox, Michael Trubshawe, Eugene Deckers, Moultrie Kelsall, Christopher Hewett, Marie Ney, and John Warwick.

CREDITS
Director: Charles Crichton; *Producer*: Michael Balcon; *Screenwriter*: T. E. B. Clarke; *Cinematographer*: Douglas Slocombe; *Editor*: Seth Holt; *Art Director*: William Kellner; *Music*: Georges Auric; *Running time*: 78 minutes. Available on videocassette and laser disc.

ORIGINAL RELEASE
1951; a General Film Distributors release of an Ealing Studios production. *U.S. Distributor*: Universal-International.

THE FILM
Released in Britain only a month after *Young Wives' Tale*, this classic Alec Guinness comedy was obviously produced earlier, when Audrey Hepburn was only too willing to accept a one-line bit part in a prestige picture like *The Lavender Hill Mob*.

It's all about a mild-mannered bank clerk who, after twenty years of honest service, plots the perfect robbery, heisting a fortune in gold bullion, to be melted down into Eiffel Tower paperweights and smuggled out of the country. But on a field trip to Paris, English schoolgirls manage to bring back six of these golden "souvenirs," and the authorities start tracking Guinness's bumbling, four-member "mob."

This most delightfully droll of all caper films won

a Hollywood Oscar for T. E. B. Clarke's original script, and a Best Screenplay prize at the 1951 Venice Film Festival. In its own country, *The Lavender Hill Mob* was voted that year's Best British Film by the British Film Academy.

Audrey Hepburn's fleeting appearance occurs in the Rio de Janeiro setting that frames the picture, as a fugitive Guinness, seated in a restaurant, recounts his story to a companion. As a pretty young thing named Chiquita, she suddenly materializes at his side to accept a generous monetary gift and his advice to "get yourself a little birthday present." Leaning over to kiss his cheek, she responds with "Oh, but how sweet of you! Thank you." And she disappears.

CRITICS' CIRCLE

"The ingenious starting-point of T. E. B. Clarke's script of *The Lavender Hill Mob* provides some episodes of original and diverting comedy, and allows Alec Guinness and Stanley Holloway to develop two characterizations in lovely contrast. During the second half of the film the writer's facility for mechanical contrivance runs away with him, in a series of over-gagged scenes; and Charles Crichton's direction strains too much for farce."

—Gavin Lambert, *Sight and Sound*

"Guinness, as usual, shines . . . and is at his best as the mastermind plotting the intricate details of the crime. Holloway is an excellent aide, while the two professional crooks in the gang, Sidney James and Alfie Bass, complete the quartet with an abundance of cockney humor."

—"Myro.," *Variety*

"Amusing situations and dialogue are well paced and sustained throughout; the climax is delightful."

—*Monthly Film Bulletin*

"That genius for civilized humor possessed by Britain's Ealing Studios, where they have tossed off such dexterous rib-ticklers as *Passport to Pimlico* and *Kind Hearts and Coronets*, has been wound up again and set humming in a jolly trifle called *The Lavender Hill Mob*. And once again Alec Guinness, who played eight roles in *Kind Hearts and Coronets*, delivers himself of one character that is as wickedly droll as Halloween."

—Bosley Crowther, *New York Times*

THE LAVENDER HILL MOB
With Alec Guinness and
unidentified player

Secret People

CAST

Valentina Cortesa (*Maria Brent/Lena Collins*); Serge Reggiani (*Louis/Gregor*); Audrey Hepburn (*Nora Brent*); Charles Goldner (*Anselmo*); Megs Jenkins (*Penny*); Irene Worth (*Miss Jackson*); Reginald Tate (*Inspector Eliot*); Michael Shepley (*Manager*); Athene Seyler (*Mrs. Kellick*); Geoffrey Hibbert (*Steenie*); Sydney Tafler (*Syd Burnett*); John Ruddock (*Daly*); Michael Allan (*Rodd*); John Field (*Fedor Luki*); Norman Williams (*Sergeant/Newcombe*); Bob Monkhouse (*Barber*); Charles Cairoli & Paul (*Specialty Act*).

CREDITS

Director: Thorold Dickinson; *Producer*: Sidney Cole; *Screenwriters*: Thorold Dickinson, Wolfgang Wilhelm, and Christianna Brand; *Based on a story by* Thorold Dickinson and Joyce Carey; *Cinematographer*; Gordon Dines; *Editor*: Peter Tanner; *Art Director*: William Kellner; *Music*: Roberto Gerhard; *Running time*: 96 minutes.

ORIGINAL RELEASE

1952; a General Film Distributors release of an Ealing Studios production. *U.S. Distributor*: Lippert Pictures.

THE FILM

Audrey Hepburn was accorded third billing, just under nominal stars Valentina Cortesa and Serge Reggiani, in this murky little drama that came and went with little notice early in 1952. Its American release in August of that year undoubtedly came about due to interest in its distaff star, whose surname had been altered from Cortese to Cortesa during a brief Hollywood sojourn in such late-forties/early-fifties melodramas as *Malaya*, *Thieves' Highway*, and *The House on Telegraph Hill*.

Set in thirties London, *Secret People* centers on an assassination plot involving political exiles and old lovers Maria (Cortesa) and Louis (Reggiani) from an unspecified European country who target a dictator

77

SECRET PEOPLE With
Charles Goldner and
Valentina Cortesa

SECRET PEOPLE   With Valentina Cortesa and Serge Reggiani

(responsible for the death of her father) during his visit to Britain. The movie's best sequence centers on the planting of a bomb, during a party honoring the dictator, while Maria's younger sister Nora (Hepburn) distracts those present by dancing in the evening's entertainment. But their plot misfires, and in the subsequent explosion, only an innocent waitress is killed. Later, Maria sacrifices herself to save her sister.

Aside from affording Audrey Hepburn an opportunity to display her early dancing skills, *Secret People* allowed her more footage than heretofore. Despite formidable competition from Cortesa (an actress of talent perhaps second only to Anna Magnani in her native Italy), the fledgling Hepburn starts to blossom with the unique blend of inner beauty, outer glow, and incandescent vulnerability that attracts audience attention whenever she's on-screen. Unfortunately, her British-sounding speech patterns contrasted oddly with the Italianated English of her screen sister.

CRITICS' CIRCLE

"Here is one of the most disappointing efforts to come from Ealing Studios in some time. *Secret People* is a hackneyed story of political agents working against a tyrannical dictator, dressed up with all the familiar clichés to make a dull and rather confusing offering. It has only remote possibilities for the American market.

"The sinister backroom plotting against the dictator is handled with an over-heavy touch. The subject lacks realism, and the only genuine suspense in the story is a tense sixty seconds waiting for a time-bomb to explode.

"Valentina Cortesa, restricted by the inadequacies of the story, doesn't register with conviction. Serge Reggiani, as her former friend, is far too obviously drawn as the sinister and callous agent. Audrey Hepburn, in a minor role as the kid sister, combines beauty with skill, particularly in two short dance sequences."

—"Myro.," *Variety*

"The expressive camera movements and editing technique of director Thorold Dickinson were much discussed at the time, yet the film isn't very gripping.

"With the young Audrey Hepburn in a sizable role, it's rather like seeing Cinderella before the transformation."

—Pauline Kael, *5001 Nights at the Movies*

"The drama is slackly constructed, but interesting; alas, it pleased few members of the critics or the public."

—David Quinlan, *British Sound Films*

SECRET PEOPLE With Valentina Cortesa

MONTE CARLO BABY With Marcel Dalio and unidentified player

Nous irons á Monte Carlo

(WE WILL GO TO MONTE CARLO)

(FRENCH VERSION OF *MONTE CARLO BABY*—SEE BELOW)

CAST
Philippe Lemaire (*Philippe*); Danielle Godet (*Jacqueline*); Henri Genes (*Antoine*); Jeanette Batti (*Marinette*); Audrey Hepburn (*Melissa Walter*); Marcel Dalio (*Poulos*); Ray Ventura and His Orchestra (*Themselves*); Max Elloy (*Max*); Andre Luguet (*Chatenay-Maillart*); Georges Lannes (*Private Detective*); John Van Dreelen (*Rudy Walter*); Y. Orrigo (*Baby*).

CREDITS
Director: Jean Boyer; *Producer*: Ray Ventura; *Screenwriters*: Jean Boyer, Alex Joffe and Serge Veber; *Cinematographer*: Charles Suin; *Editor*: Franchette Mazin; *Art Director*: Robert Giordani; *Music*: Paul Misraki; *Running time*: 89 minutes.

ORIGINAL RELEASE
1952; a Corona release of an Hoche production.

MONTE CARLO BABY With Marcel Dalio

MONTE CARLO BABY   With
Marcel Dalio

Monte Carlo Baby

(BABY BEATS THE BAND)

(English version of *Nous irons à Monte Carlo*)

CAST
Audrey Hepburn (*Linda Farrell*); Jules Munshin (*Antoine*); Michele Farmer (*Jacqueline*); Cara Williams (*Marinette*); Philippe Lemaire (*Philippe*); Russell Collins (*Max*); Ray Ventura and His Orchestra (*Themselves*).

CREDITS
Directors: Jean Boyer and Lester Fuller; *Producer*: Ray Ventura; *Screenwriters*: Alex Joffe, Jean Boyer, and Lester Fuller; *Cinematographer*: Charles Suin; *Editor*: Fanchette Mazin; *Art Director*: Robert Giordani; *Music*: Paul Misraki; *Songs*: Paul Misraki and Geoffrey Parsons; *Running time*: 79 minutes.

ORIGINAL RELEASE
1953; *U.S. Distributor*: Favorite Pictures (1954).

THE FILM
Audrey Hepburn's last European-made film before stardom rescued her forever from this sort of thing

81

was a trivial farce, shot in both French and English versions. And although there were some cast changes to accommodate the language barrier, Hepburn's facility with French enabled her to be cast in both *Nous irons à Monte Carlo* and *Monte Carlo Baby*. When the latter was accorded a belated post–*Roman Holiday* U.S. release in mid-1954, she was understandably top-billed over Jules Munshin, Michele Farmer, and Cara Williams. However, her supporting role, as an actress who occasionally pops in and out amidst this foolish little comedy about a lost infant, made little impact. Indeed, had the location shooting not led to a momentous chance meeting with the legendary French writer Colette—and subsequently the Broadway adaptation of *Gigi*—the name of Audrey Hepburn might never have found fame and fortune.

CRITICS' CIRCLE

"The film devoted too much time to a contrived comedy of errors about a misplaced baby that involves a series of chases, mistaken identities and double entendres. While unpretentious, this might get by in lower-case spots or some dualers in the U.S."

—"Mosk.," *Variety*

"Though nominally the star, Audrey Hepburn . . . has very little to do as the baby's real mother. The baby itself appears understandably bewildered at its participation in this rather poor grown-up joke."

—*Monthly Film Bulletin*

"*Monte Carlo Baby*, as witless a film exercise as ever was spewed from an ingenious camera, blared into the Palace yesterday. Blared is the proper word, for most of the dialogue and action . . . is screamed at the poor spectators in an unceasing clamor. Perhaps all the frenetic rushing about is designed to cover up the pointless plot of a missing baby (diapered version) in the custody of Ray Ventura's band.

"Jules Munshin apes and grimaces offensively throughout. Cara Williams races breathlessly through the film, acting remarkably as though she didn't know what to do or say next. Audrey Hepburn appears in it occasionally, playing a movie star. She made this one before she became one in reality. It is rather astonishing how she stands out in that seared desert of mediocrity. Miss Hepburn saves *Monte Carlo Baby* from being completely worthless."

—Oscar Godbout, *New York Times*

MONTE CARLO BABY With Cara Williams

Roman Holiday

CAST

Gregory Peck (*Joe Bradley*); Audrey Hepburn (*Princess Anne*); Eddie Albert (*Irving Radovich*); Hartley Power (*Mr. Hennessy*); Laura Solari (*Hennessy's Secretary*); Harcourt Williams (*Ambassador*); Margaret Rawlings (*Countess Vereberg*); Tullio Carminati (*General Provno*); Paolo Carlini (*Mario Delani*); Claudio Ermelli (*Giovanni*); Paola Borboni (*Charwoman*); Heinz Hindrich (*Dr. Bonnachoven*); Gorella Gori (*Shoe Seller*); Alfredo Rizzo (*Taxi Driver*); John Horne (*Master of Ceremonies*); Eric Oulton (*Sir Hugo Macy de Farmington*).

CREDITS

Producer-Director: William Wyler; *Associate Producer*: Robert Wyler; *Screenwriter*: Dalton Trumbo (*but officially credited to* Ian McLellan Hunter and John Dighton); *Based on a story by* Dalton Trumbo (*officially credited to* Hunter); *Cinematographers*: Franz F. Planer and Henri Alekan; *Editor*: Robert Swink; *Art Directors*: Hal Pereira and Walter Tyler; *Music*: Georges Auric; *Running time*: 119 minutes. Available on videocassette and laser disc.

ORIGINAL RELEASE

1953; a Paramount Picture.

THE FILM

Audrey Hepburn's international breakthrough came about because producer-director William Wyler was seeking a little-known non-American-accented actress who could believably portray a young European princess, opposite Gregory Peck, in *Roman Holiday*.

The movie's delightful screenplay—credited to John Dighton and Ian McLellan Hunter, but much

83

ROMAN HOLIDAY   As Princess Anne

later revealed to have been written by the blacklisted Dalton Trumbo—had originally been on filmmaker Frank Capra's agenda in the forties, when he planned to borrow Elizabeth Taylor from MGM to team with Cary Grant in a Liberty Films production for RKO. But the director's initial Liberty projects, *It's a Wonderful Life* and *State of the Union*, proved disappointing at the box office, and the production company Capra shared with George Stevens, William Wyler, and Sam Briskin was sold to Paramount, along with its literary properties. Among these was *Roman Holiday*, which Capra then hoped to film under that studio's logo—until he ran up against a Paramount ruling that no picture could be budgeted above $1.5 million. Unable to comply, Capra abandoned *Roman Holiday*, which went to William Wyler, directing his first non-dramatic movie since the thirties. He insisted the film be shot on location in Rome, which was fine with Paramount, since the company had blocked funds in Italy and wanted to use those lire for this production. Wyler's once-voiced regret was that he hadn't planned for Technicolor. "I tried to switch," Wyler recalled to his biographer, Axel Madsen, "but in those days making pictures in color was unusual. I would have needed new film stock, had to fly exposed film every day to London, and reorganize the production. It was just too late."

Initially, *Roman Holiday*'s big-name star, Gregory Peck, turned it down, on the grounds that the leading female role of Princess Anne—who temporarily forsakes her royal duties to experience life and love during a state visit to the Eternal City—was the movie's more important role and likely to overshadow that of the American journalist who romances her.

Wyler's response employed subtle psychology: "You surprise me. If you didn't like the story, okay, but because somebody else's part is a little better than yours, well, that's no reason to turn down a film. I didn't think you were the kind of actor who measures the size of the roles." Peck met the challenge, and Wyler began searching for his Princess Anne. For a time, British-born Jean Simmons, then under contract to Howard Hughes, was the prime contender. But lengthy negotiations with Hughes reached a stalemate over his price for her services.

En route to Italy for preproduction business, Wyler visited London to interview several possible candidates, among them Audrey Hepburn, who now had seven films to her credit, as well as stage experience.

ROMAN HOLIDAY   As Princess Anne

ROMAN HOLIDAY   With Gregory Peck

The slim twenty-three-year-old impressed the film-maker with her poise, charm, and quiet beauty. Determining that this was a "class act" worthy of consideration, Wyler ordered a screen test for the actress, advising test director Thorold Dickinson (*Secret People*) to trick Hepburn, after completion of her scene, by keeping his camera rolling after calling "cut." By so doing, he could observe her natural reactions, in addition to her further reaction when she realized she was still being photographed.

"That was the film we received in Rome," Wyler remembered. "Acting, looks, and personality! She was absolutely enchanting, and we said, 'That's the girl!' After so many drive-in waitresses becoming movie stars, there has been this real drought, when along comes class; somebody who actually went to school, can spell, maybe even plays the piano. She may be a wispy, thin little thing, but when you see that girl, you know you're really in the presence of something. In that league there's only ever been Garbo, and

ROMAN HOLIDAY   With Paolo Carlini

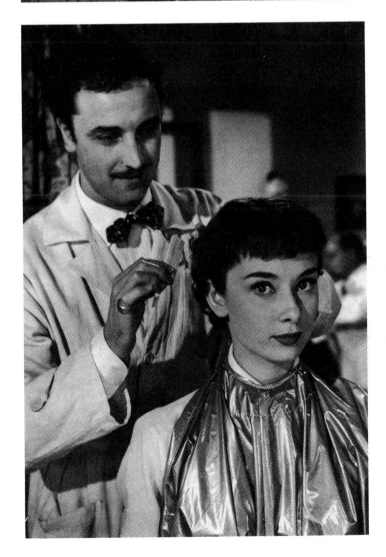

ROMAN HOLIDAY   With Gregory Peck

ROMAN HOLIDAY   With Gregory Peck

ROMAN HOLIDAY   With
Eddie Albert and
Gregory Peck

the other Hepburn, and maybe Bergman. It's a rare quality, but boy, do you know when you've found it." However, filming couldn't begin until after the actress had fulfilled her commitment to appear on Broadway in *Gigi*. And although Wyler doubted that the play would last, it ran six months and finally had to close while continuing to sell out. Contractual arrangements permitted Audrey Hepburn to leave *Gigi* only for the

ROMAN HOLIDAY   With Gregory Peck

movie, and she agreed to rejoin the play afterward for a national road tour.

Roman Holiday offers a Cinderella story in reverse. Constantly advised, overprotected, and serious beyond her years, Princess Anne tours Europe's capitals, obediently making the expected public appearances. But in Rome, she evades her protectors and sneaks out at night to discover how the ordinary Romans live. Exhausted from a rigorous schedule, she falls asleep in a public place, where she meets journalist Joe Bradley (Peck) and photographer Irving Radovich (Eddie Albert). Recognizing the young lady, Bradley at first charms her for the exclusive story he visualizes writing. But after (innocently) sharing his quarters with her that night, he finds he's falling in love, and selfish thoughts dissipate as they experience Rome together. The princess not only lets down her long tresses, but also gets a more fashionable cut, as she blossoms to embrace a man—and a way of life— she knows she cannot keep. At the movie's close,

having reluctantly resumed her appointed duties, she faces Joe and Irving at a dignified press conference where they can only verbalize their feelings about their mutual Roman holiday in guarded formalities.

Roman Holiday won glowing notices and became an immediate hit when it opened in the late summer of 1953 at New York's vast Radio City Music Hall. Gregory Peck's initial perception that it was an actress's vehicle was officially confirmed. Nominated for no less than ten Academy Awards, it brought Paramount Pictures three Oscars—for Best Actress Audrey Hepburn, Edith Head's costume designs, and

ROMAN HOLIDAY   With Gregory Peck

ROMAN HOLIDAY   As Princess Anne

the original story by "Ian McLellan Hunter." The New York Film Critics Circle named Hepburn 1953's Best Actress. Unexpectedly serving as prepublicity for *Roman Holiday* during its 1952 production was the real-life conflict between love and royal obligation that split Britain's Princess Margaret and Group Captain Peter Townsend.

Hepburn generally enjoyed a smooth working relationship with her director. But there was a crucial scene of parting between Peck and Hepburn in which the actress couldn't simulate emotion—that is, until the demanding Wyler ran out of patience and brought his star to tears with words of angry exasperation. In Gregory Peck's words: "It was embarrassing and frightened her and shook her up, but she did it perfectly the very next time. On screen it looked like it was because she was parting from me, but actually it was because Wyler had just scared the wits out of her."

The experience failed to keep Hepburn and Wyler from teaming together twice more for *The Children's Hour* (1962) and *How to Steal a Million* (1966).

In 1987, NBC had the misguided notion of remaking *Roman Holiday* as a television movie, starring Tom Conti, Catherine Oxenberg, and Ed Begley Jr., in the respective Peck, Hepburn, and Albert roles.

ROMAN HOLIDAY   With Gregory Peck and Eddie Albert

In the opinion of one national critic, this was "not even a reasonable facsimile" of the original.

CRITICS' CIRCLE

"It is a contrived fable but a bittersweet legend with laughs that leaves the spirits soaring. Call *Roman Holiday* a credit to William Wyler's versatility. The producer-director, who has been expanding his not inconsiderable talents on worthy but serious themes, is herein trying on the mantle of the late Ernst Lubitsch and making it fit fairly well.

"Although she is not precisely a newcomer to films, Audrey Hepburn, the British actress who is being starred for the first time as Princess Anne, is a slender, elfin and wistful beauty, alternately regal and childlike in her profound appreciation of newly found simple pleasures and love. Although she bravely smiles her acknowledgment of the end of that affair, she remains a pitifully lonely figure facing a stiff future. Gregory Peck makes a stalwart and manly escort and lover, whose eyes belie his restrained exterior."

—A. H. Weiler, *New York Times*

"What Wyler has done is to fashion one of the gayest, most original and endearing comedies to be credited to Hollywood in recent years."

—*Newsweek*

"This is Wyler's first venture into comedy in many years and the switch from the heavy dramas he has been associated with since 1935 is all to the good. The aged face of the Eternal City provides a contrast to the picture's introduction of a new face, Audrey Hepburn, British ingenue who already has made an impression with legit-goers in *Gigi*. The young lady has talent, plus a personality that wears well on film. She has a delightful affectation in voice and delivery that is controlled just enough to have charm and serve as a trademark, as well as the looks and poise to make her role of a princess of a not-too-mythical country come over strongly."

—"Brog.," *Variety*

"Amid the rhinestone glitter of *Roman Holiday*'s make-believe, Paramount's new star sparkles and glows with the fire of a finely cut diamond."

—*Time*

"There is absolutely nothing uncommon about its plot, yet a capable director and a remarkable young actress have made one of the better pictures of the year, certainly one of the brightest comedies. Hepburn makes the sad skylarking of a princess lovely and carries off the finale with a nicety that leaves one a little haunted."

—Otis L. Guernsey Jr., *New York Herald Tribune*

"This is the picture that made Audrey Hepburn a movie star. Probably no one could have brought out her skinny, long-necked gamine magic as winningly as the director William Wyler did; his calm, elegant style prepares the scenes and builds the character until she has the audience enthralled, and when she smiles we're all goners."

—Pauline Kael, *5001 Nights at the Movies*

"*Roman Holiday* is a lacy mixture of frothy fun and bittersweet emotion, with plot . . . the least of the matter. Televising, therefore, spoils the story by interruptions; and while it doesn't improve the making of mood or weaving of spell, it does let us see the lovely fragility and haunting charm that marked Audrey Hepburn in her Oscar-winning American screen debut, and the fine complement Gregory Peck provides in both comedy and compassion."

—Judith Crist, *TV Guide*

Sabrina

(SABRINA FAIR)

SABRINA   As Sabrina Fairchild

CAST
Humphrey Bogart (*Linus Larrabee*); Audrey Hepburn (*Sabrina Fairchild*); William Holden (*David Larrabee*); Walter Hampden (*Oliver Larrabee*); John Williams (*Thomas Fairchild*); Martha Hyer (*Elizabeth Tyson*); Joan Vohs (*Gretchen Van Horn*); Marcel Dalio (*Baron*); Marcell Hillaire (*The Professor*); Nella Walker (*Maude Larrabee*); Francis X. Bushman (*Mr. Tyson*); Ellen Corby (*Miss McCardle*); Marjorie Bennett (*Margaret, the Cook*); Emory Parnell (*Charles, the Butler*); Kay Riehl (*Mrs. Tyson*); Nancy Kulp (*Jenny, the Maid*); Kay Kuter (*Houseman*); Paul Harvey (*Doctor*); Emmett Vogan and Colin Campbell (*Board Members*).

CREDITS
Producer-Director: Billy Wilder; *Screenwriters*: Billy Wilder, Samuel Taylor, and Ernest Lehman; *Based on the play* Sabrina Fair *by* Samuel Taylor; *Cinematographer*: Charles Lang Jr.; *Editor*: Arthur Schmidt; *Art Directors*: Hal Pereira and Walter Tyler; *Set Decorators*: Sam Comer and Ray Moyer; *Costumes*: Edith Head and (uncredited) Hubert de Givenchy; *Special Effects*: John P. Fulton and Farciot Edouart; *Music*: Frederick Hollander; *Songs*: Wilson Stone; Richard Rodgers and Lorenz Hart; Harold Lewis and John Cope; *Running time*: 114 minutes. Available on videocassette and laser disc.

ORIGINAL RELEASE
1954; a Paramount Picture.

THE FILM
Sabrina Fair, Samuel Taylor's 1953 Broadway success, had brought the charming, husky-voiced Margaret Sullavan back to the New York stage—surprisingly successfully, for at forty-four she still looked youthful enough to get away with playing a young woman in her early twenties!

Acquiring this hit comedy for the movies, producer-director Billy Wilder cast the title role more appropriately, with Audrey Hepburn as the Long Island chauffeur's daughter, who ages from nineteen to twenty-one during the film, the title of which was abbreviated (except in Britain) to a mere *Sabrina*. However, the twenty-four-year-old Hepburn's leading men would have been more suitable opposite Sullavan, with William Holden (thirty-six) as her employer's irresponsible "young" playboy son and Humphrey Bogart (fifty-five) as his soberly work-oriented older brother. Wilder had intended the latter role for Cary Grant (forty-nine), who declined to play a "stuffy businessman," so Bogart was a last-minute replacement. It wasn't a happy arrangement; Bogie didn't like the picture or William Holden or Billy Wilder. In turn, Wilder had little use for the irascible, impatient Bogie—who also griped about the less-experienced Hepburn's need for many "takes" to get her scenes right. Bogart's compensation: he got top billing, and he got the girl, belief-suspending though it may have been.

Playwright Samuel Taylor collaborated with Billy Wilder and Ernest Lehman on this adaptation of Taylor's play, which lost some subsidiary characters and gained others. And it was "opened up" to allow for the Parisian sequence where Sabrina grows from awkward teenager to a chic, sophisticated twenty-one, as she

SABRINA   As Sabrina Fairchild

SABRINA   With Humphrey Bogart

SABRINA   With William Holden

studies Cordon Bleu cooking. Actually, the film begins prior to the play, which opens with the young woman's return from Paris. But most of the picture takes place on the posh Long Island estate of the Larrabees, where Sabrina has long adored the handsome and carefree son David (Holden), despite his two failed marriages and dissolute lifestyle.

A carbon-monoxide suicide attempt had not only failed to win Sabrina his attentions, but had occasioned her being sent away to France "to forget David." But her return with a new look intrigues David, who doesn't recognize her as the all-grown-up offspring of the Larrabee chauffeur, Fairchild (John Williams). But now David is engaged to the equally well-to-do Elizabeth Tyson (Martha Hyer), and brother Linus (Bogart) soon determines that Sabrina must not interfere with that match, so he pretends to court her himself. In so doing, of course he falls in love with her. And since this is little more than a simple Cinderella fairy tale, we must presume that the doelike young Hepburn and crusty old Bogart somehow live happily ever after.

With its starring trio of recent Oscar winners and Billy Wilder's box-office touch, *Sabrina* could hardly lose. Despite its black-and-white conventionalities, the film was enthusiastically received by the majority of the critics and the moviegoing public. Paramount realized impressive profits from the picture. The recipient of six Academy Award nominations, including Audrey Hepburn for Best Actress and Billy Wilder for Best Director, *Sabrina* received only one statuette, which, ironically enough, went to designer Edith Head—whose hollow triumph owed much to the gorgeous ball gown provided for Hepburn by an uncredited Givenchy!

A new version of *Sabrina*, starring Harrison Ford, Julia Ormond, and television personality Greg Kinnear, premiered in fall 1995.

CRITICS' CIRCLE

"*Sabrina* is, in our wistful estimation, the most delightful comedy-romance in years. One might guess this is Miss Hepburn's picture, since she has the title role and has come to it trailing her triumphs from last year's *Roman Holiday*. And, indeed, she is wonderful in it—a young lady of extraordinary range of sensitive and moving expressions within such a frail and slender frame. She is even more luminous as the daughter and pet of the servants hall than she was as a princess last year, and no more than that can be said.

"But credit, above all, Mr. Wilder, for it is his unerring sense of form, his fluency with the picture, his feel for the realistic look, his dramatic use of popular music and his wonderfully hard grained comic style that makes *Sabrina* a picture to be cherished as a real and lasting joy."

—Bosley Crowther, *New York Times*

"Actress Hepburn's appeal, it becomes clearer with every appearance, is largely to the imagination; the less acting she does, the more people can imagine her doing, and wisely she does very little in *Sabrina*. That little she does skillfully. By contrast, actor Holden seems almost too true to a banal type to be good. Bogart, however, being as much of a symbol as Hepburn is—and a cunning scene-stealer besides—holds his own with ease, and sometimes sets little Audrey down, toreador pants and all, as a Vogue model who has risen above her station."

Time

"Audrey Hepburn appears, at the moment, an original personality rather than a fully accomplished player: William Wyler's discreet and skillful handling in *Roman Holiday* exploited her particular quality—naïveté combined with poise—to the full; Wilder's less flexible treatment makes demands which she is not altogether capable of meeting."

"P. H.," *Monthly Film Bulletin*

"*Sabrina* is the prick that bursts the fair bubble that was Audrey Hepburn in *Roman Holiday*. Surely the vogue for sexuality can go no further than this weird hybrid with butchered hair. Of course, none of this would really matter if the charm and grace were sincere, but I am afraid that she is letting her calculation show. The toothy grins are pure Ann Blyth and the coo-ings are a direct borrowing from Joan Greenwood."

—*Films and Filming*

"Audrey Hepburn is forced to overdo her gamine charm in this horrible concoction about a Cinderella among the Long Island rich."

—Pauline Kael, *5001 Nights at the Movies*

SABRINA With
William Holden

SABRINA With John
Williams

SABRINA With
Humphrey Bogart

93

SABRINA   With William Holden

"A slick blend of heart and chuckles makes *Sabrina* a sock romantic comedy that should catch on at the boxoffice and rate hearty ticket sales.

"The fun is in the playing. Bogart is sock as the tycoon with no time for gals until he gets Miss Hepburn's mind off Holden. The latter sells his comedy strongly, wrapping up a character somewhat offbeat for him. Miss Hepburn again demonstrates a winning talent for being 'Miss Cinderella' and will have audiences rooting for her all the way."

"Brog.," *Variety*

SABRINA   As Sabrina Fairchild

SABRINA   With Humphrey Bogart

SABRINA   As Sabrina Fairchild in her Givenchy gown

95

diff; *Second-Unit Photography*: Aldo Tonti; *Editors*: Stuart Gilmore and Leo Catozzo; *Art Directors*: Mario Chiari, Franz Bachelin, and Gianni Polidori; *Set Decorator*: Piero Gherardi; *Costumes*: Maria de Matteis; *Music*: Nino Rota; *Running time*: 208 minutes. Available on videocassette and laser disc.

War and Peace

CAST

Audrey Hepburn (*Natasha Rostov*); Henry Fonda (*Pierre Bezukhov*); Mel Ferrer (*Prince Andrei Bolkonsky*); Vittorio Gassman (*Anatole Kuragin*); John Mills (*Platon Karatsev*); Herbert Lom (*Napoleon*); Oscar Homolka (*Gen. Mikhail Kutuzov*); Anita Ekberg (*Helene*); Helmut Dantine (*Dolokhov*); Barry Jones (*Count Ilya Rostov*); Anna Maria Ferrero (*Mary Bolkonsky*); Milly Vitale (*Lise Bolkonsky*); Jeremy Brett (*Nicholas Rostov*); Lea Seidl (*Countess Rostov*); Wilfred Lawson (*Prince Nicholas Bolkonsky*); Sean Barrett (*Petya Rostov*); Tullio Carminati (*Prince Vasili Kuragin*); May Britt (*Sonya Rostov*); Patrick Crean (*Vasili Denisov*); Gertrude Flynn (*Peronskaya*); Teresa Pellati (*Masa*); Marisa Allasio (*Matriosa, Dolokhov's Servant*); Giacomo Rossi-Stuart (*Young Cossack*).

CREDITS

Directors: King Vidor and (uncredited) Mario Soldati (battle scenes); *Producer*: Dino De Laurentiis (for Ponti–De Laurentiis Productions); *Screenwriters*: Bridget Boland, Robert Westerby, King Vidor, Mario Camerini, Ennio de Concini, Ivo Perilli, and (uncredited) Irwin Shaw; *Based on the novel by* Leo Tolstoy; *VistaVision-Technicolor Cinematographer*: Jack Car-

ORIGINAL RELEASE
1956; a Paramount release of a Ponti–De Laurentiis production.

THE FILM
Lev Nikolayevich Tolstoy's vast, panoramic story of

WAR AND PEACE   As Natasha Rostov

With Mel Ferrer in *War and Peace* (1956)

WAR AND PEACE   With May Britt and Jeremy Brett

aristocratic Russian interrelationships and battle campaigns amid the Napoleonic Wars took six years to write (1863–69) and some might say about as long to read! Many consider this the greatest novel ever written. It was first brought to the screen by the Russians in 1916. In the late thirties, Alexander

97

WAR AND PEACE   As Natasha Rostov

team of Carlo Ponti and Dino De Laurentiis, in alliance with Paramount Pictures, inaugurated their own production first, under the direction of Hollywood veteran King Vidor.

At a cost of more than $6 million, they achieved a three-and-a-half-hour condensation (edited down from a first cut of five hours) of Tolstoy that reduced the author's twenty-three principal characters to seventeen and his ten original battles to three. And the story emphasis was shifted from the mystical Pierre to romance-minded Natasha. *War and Peace* was largely filmed at Rome's Cinecittà studios, with battle scenes and some exteriors shot in the Italian Alps and Yugoslavia. Heading its international (and partially dubbed) cast were Audrey Hepburn, Henry Fonda, and Mel Ferrer. Not a few critics seemed to agree with director Vidor's comment at the end of filming: "Audrey Hepburn *is* Natasha. She is fresh out of the book. I know of no other actress who could have played the part. I liked working with Audrey Hepburn tremendously."

In 1967, the Russians completed *Voina i mir*, a spectacular version of *War and Peace* that was then the longest and costliest motion picture ever made, at a government-supported cost reportedly in the neighborhood of $100 million. In production for five years, it was initially shown in the Soviet Union in four separate parts, totaling some seven hours and thirteen minutes. It was directed by actor Sergei Bondarchuk, who also played the leading role of Pierre. Shown in the United States in a somewhat edited, two-part, English-dubbed version, that *War and Peace* was named Best Foreign Film of 1968 by the New York Film Critics, the National Board of Review, and the Academy of Motion Picture Arts and Sciences.

The Russian *War and Peace* may stand as the definitive adaptation of Tolstoy, but its length and inadequate dubbing contribute to its relative international obscurity in the nineties. Thus, King Vidor's version, which remains available to the consumer in a beautifully Technicolored videocassette, currently stands as the most accessible *War and Peace* for English-speaking audiences. Incidentally, its cinematography won a 1956 Oscar nomination for Jack Cardiff.

CRITICS' CIRCLE

"This timeless and changeless progression through the episodes of Tolstoy's cluttered tale make for an

Korda repeatedly announced plans to produce a British film version, first to star his wife, Merle Oberon, and Laurence Olivier, then, in the mid-forties, in a coproduction with Metro-Goldwyn-Mayer. The latter was to have Orson Welles acting opposite Oberon, in addition to serving as director and coproducer. Undoubtedly, World War II made its production costs impossible. Nor was David O. Selznick (in search of a follow-up to *Gone With the Wind*) able to solve the problem of expense when he announced similar plans to film *War and Peace* in the early fifties. Subsequently, showman Mike Todd was scheduled to produce an adaptation of Tolstoy's novel with Fred Zinnemann as director. But in Italy, the rival production

WAR AND PEACE   With
Lea Seidl, Barry Jones,
May Britt, Henry Fonda,
and Sean Barrett

WAR AND PEACE   With May
Britt, Lea Seidl, Mel Ferrer,
and Henry Fonda

WAR AND PEACE   With
Sean Barrett, Henry
Fonda, and Mel Ferrer

WAR AND PEACE   With Anita Ekberg and Vittorio Gassman

WAR AND PEACE   As Natasha Rostov

oddly mechanical and emotionally sterile air. The characters seem second-rate people, hackneyed and without much depth. There are sequences and moments of fire and beauty, and certainly the mighty spectacles of clashing armies and Napoleon's retreat from Moscow are pictorially impressive and exciting beyond words. But, alas, the human stories that Tolstoy told so significantly in the book are sketchy and inconsequential, despite the time devoted to them. Naturally, Pierre and Natasha emerge as the focal characters, but neither is intense nor meaningful. Natasha, played by Miss Hepburn, is charmingly girlish [but her] amorous infatuations with Prince Andrei and the leering Anatole are represented without warmth. Indeed, the critical surrender to Anatole, whom Vittorio Gassman plays with lips and eyes, is

completely unmotivated. This is the saddest single flaw in the film."

—Bosley Crowther, *New York Times*

"Audrey Hepburn, as Natasha, has the irresistible radiance of youth. She is very beautiful and she has a shining exuberance. At the end there is a maturity about her, a compassion, that is very touching. And yet she has not lost the gaiety that was so captivating when she was young and life was a game. This is a

WAR AND PEACE   With Mel Ferrer

WAR AND PEACE   With Barry Jones

101

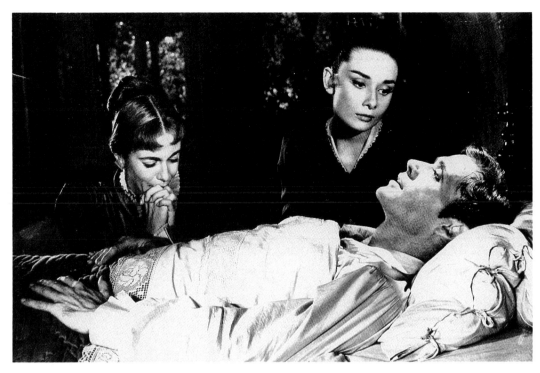

WAR AND PEACE With Milly Vitale and Mel Ferrer

WAR AND PEACE With Henry Fonda

rare and subtle feat of acting. A fleeting look in her eyes can express all the pain of growing up. Certainly it is the best feminine performance of the year."

—William K. Zinsser, *New York Herald Tribune*

"A visual epic that is assured of permanent stature in the annals of the motion picture industry. *War and Peace* is a real blockbuster. It is a rich contribution to the art form of the picture business in the best tradition. The greater wonder is that such a monumental work could be condensed to three and a half hours. The wonder of the De Laurentiis–Vidor production is that it has maintained cohesiveness and fluidity of story and also has given fullest accent to the size and sweep of Bonaparte's armies at Austerlitz and Borodino.

"Audrey Hepburn is the epitome of wholesome young love under benevolent aristocratic rearing. Henry Fonda . . . is perhaps sometimes too literally the confused character. Other than the above and the moody but compelling performance by Mel Ferrer, the rest are lesser roles but almost wholly effective."

—"Abel.," *Variety*

"Of the film's three stars, only Audrey Hepburn, with her precocious child's head set up on a swanlike neck, looks the part. She is perfectly the Natasha described by Tolstoy. In her playing, Audrey catches the gamine qualities of Natasha and her softness. What is lacking is the steely courage that would let Natasha brand her flesh with a red-hot iron to prove her love. Instead of a total commitment to life, there is more often a quiet acceptance of fate. Mel Ferrer's Prince Andrei has a certain sullen grandeur, but his diction is often unclear, and he is more wooden than reserved, more testy than proud."

—Time

"The first half of this colossal film lasts something like a hundred minutes—the length, in fact, of a normal full-length feature. Frankly, the first half is poor from almost every point of view. The dialogue is turgid. One is painfully conscious of how ill-sorted are nearly all the actors—a polyglot bunch who seem to have met each other by accident two minutes beforehand. Some are dubbed. Some are not. Despite the magnificence of the costumes and the expensive pictorial values, there is but little impression of authenticity or conviction.

"With the retreat from Moscow, *War and Peace* stirs thrillingly to life, and director King Vidor comes into his own. Scene after scene now breathes with the bitterness of defeat and despair, and one watches history on the march.

"It is difficult to judge the cast. They look dwarfed against the backgrounds, and Vidor does not appear to have given them much help, either by rehearsal or camera work. The intimate scenes fall flat.

"Audrey Hepburn looks the part of Natasha, and indeed does manage an appealing, pretty, if rather thin performance. Period stuff is not yet her forte; while her vocal mannerisms are growing unexpectedly reminiscent of the other Hepburn. Mel Ferrer is wooden; Henry Fonda, cruelly miscast with his twanging voice of a cowboy-poet echoing through Moscow.

"Simple arithmetic will inform you that Part Two also runs over a hundred minutes. Do not miss them. Those magnificent latter scenes are truly worth any filmgoer's endurance. In this version of *War and Peace*, War wins hands down."

—Peter John Dyer, *Films and Filming*

FUNNY FACE   As Jo Stockton

104

Funny Face

CAST

Audrey Hepburn (*Jo Stockton*); Fred Astaire (*Dick Avery*); Kay Thompson (*Maggie Prescott*); Michel Auclair (*Prof. Emile Flostre*); Robert Flemyng (*Paul Duval*); Dovima (*Marion*); Virginia Gibson (*Babs*); Suzy Parker and Sunny Harnett (*Dancers in "Think Pink!" Number*); Ruta Lee (*Lettie*); Alex Gerry (*Devitch*); Jean Del Val (*Hairdresser*); Iphigenie Castiglioni (*Armande*); Sue England (*Laura*); Karen Scott (*Gigi*); Diane DuBois (*Mimi*); Nesdon Booth (*Mr. Baker*); Baroness Van Heemstra and Roger Edens (*Sidewalk Cafe Patrons*).

CREDITS

Director: Stanley Donen; *Producer*: Roger Edens; *Screenwriter*: Leonard Gershe, *based on his unproduced stage musical* Wedding Day; *VistaVision-Technicolor Cinematographer*: Ray June; *Visual Consultant*: Richard Avedon; *Editor*: Frank Bracht; *Art Directors*: Hal Pereira and George W. Davis; *Costumes*: Edith Head and Hubert de Givenchy; *Music*: George Gershwin and Roger Edens; *Lyrics*: Ira Gershwin and Leonard Gershe; *Choreographer*: Eugene Loring and (uncredited) Fred Astaire and Stanley Donen; *Music Director*: Adolph Deutsch; *Orchestrations*: Con-

Posing in the Louvre in *Funny Face* (1957)

FUNNY FACE   With Kay
Thompson

FUNNY FACE   Singing
"How Long Has This
Been Going On?"

rad Salinger, Van Cleave, Alexander Courage, and
Skip Martin; *Musical Numbers*: "Think Pink!" "How
Long Has This Been Going On?" "Funny Face,"
"Bonjour, Paris!" "Basal Metabolism," "Let's Kiss
and Make Up," "He Loves and She Loves," "On How
to Be Lovely," "Marche Funèbre," "Clap Yo' Hands,"
and "'S Wonderful"; *Running time*: 103 minutes.
Available on videocassette.

ORIGINAL RELEASE
1957; a Paramount Picture.

THE FILM
With her name listed first, Audrey Hepburn shared
above-the-title billing with Fred Astaire in her first
musical picture—finally, an opportunity for the young
actress to utilize her years of dance training. In 1927,
Astaire and his sister Adele had shared a Broadway
stage with Victor Moore in a George and Ira Gershwin
musical called *Funny Face* that introduced great
songs like "My One and Only," "'S Wonderful," and
"He Loves and She Loves." But that show about an
Atlantic City jewel robbery was not the same one that
reached screens thirty years later as *Funny Face*. The
movie's Cinderella tale of a shy, intellectual bookstore
clerk (Hepburn) who's swept away into the glamorous
world of high couture by a fashion photographer (Astaire) and a chic magazine editor (Kay Thompson)
derived from an unproduced Leonard Gershe libretto

called *Wedding Day*. The man responsible for blending the Gershe "book" with the Gershwin music (and a few new numbers) was MGM's Roger Edens, who completed the package by hiring top-notch photographer Richard Avedon (on whom Astaire's Dick Avery is obviously based) to give the film its unique look and color scheme. That much of the production was set in Paris and took advantage of celebrated locations

helped set the stylish tone of a visual treat that garnered Academy Award nominations for its elegant cinematography, costume design, and art direction, as well as its charming fairy-tale screenplay.

What had begun as a prospective Metro-Goldwyn-Mayer musical ended up elsewhere when the project (Gershwin songs, Roger Edens, Leonard Gershe, and director Stanley Donen) was sold to Paramount as a

FUNNY FACE   With Fred Astaire in the title number

"Bonjour, Paris!" finishing atop the Eiffel Tower. But it's the Hepburn-Astaire duos that provide *Funny Face*'s most sublime moments, with the title song (performed in a red-filtered darkroom), "He Loves and She Loves," and "'S Wonderful"—the latter pair sung and danced against a gauzily pastoral background. Alone, Hepburn executes a Bohemian modern-ballet solo, "Basal Metabolism," and duets with Thompson to the jaunty, infectious "On How to Be Lovely."

To design her haute couture wardrobe for the Paris sequence where she's photographed as "The Quality Woman" for *Quality* (read *Vogue*) magazine, Hepburn insisted that Paramount engage Hubert de Givenchy, who had created her *Sabrina* ball gown, for which that movie's nominal designer, Edith Head, had taken official credit. With *Funny Face*, a furious Head—Paramount's top studio costumer—had to concede Audrey Hepburn's wardrobe designs to the brilliant young Frenchman, while *she* merely outfitted Kay Thompson and the supporting female cast. Most humiliating of all, Head now had to share on-screen credit with Givenchy!

FUNNY FACE   With Kay Thompson, performing "On How to Be Lovely"

vehicle for Audrey Hepburn, who had become that studio's hottest female star. Part of the arrangement also guaranteed Metro a future picture with Hepburn, who requested—and got—Fred Astaire as her partner for *Funny Face*.

The actress later confessed how frightened she was at their first meeting: "One look at this most debonair, elegant, and distinguished of legends, and I could feel myself turn to solid lead, while my heart sank into my two left feet. Then suddenly I felt a hand around my waist, and with his inimitable grace and lightness, Fred literally swept me off my feet."

The cabaret world's ultrasophisticated Kay Thompson, with her tall, angular physique and long face, makes a smashing movie debut as the film's third lead. And she even partners Astaire to great effect in the fast-stepping "Clap Yo' Hands" number. All three performers join in the complex, split-screen

CRITICS' CIRCLE

"This May-November pairing gives the Roger Edens production the benefits of Astaire's debonair style and terp accomplishments, and the sensitive acting talents of Miss Hepburn, each adding to the plot's high-style world of fashions and models."

—"Brog.," *Variety*

"A civilized, urbane entertainment, a musical bright of both manner and wit; a film not so much of spectacle as of high spirits; a musical then of incandescent charm.

"Astaire's ageless, affable charm makes for a delightful contrast with the fey gamine beauty of Miss Hepburn. He, of course, dances with disarming grace and precision, whilst she partners him with surprising agility and sings with infectious gaiety. Her 'On How to Be Lovely' song, sung with cabaret star Kay Thompson, is performed in the most scintillating style and manner.

"*Funny Face* is one of the loveliest musicals ever made. However, what really sets firm the film's total charm is a tender idyll danced by Astaire and Hepburn in the misty flower garden of a riverside church.

FUNNY FACE   As Jo Stockton, groomed as a runway model

With Kay Thompson and Fred Astaire in *Funny Face*

109

As they softly whirl through the budding daffodils and gently step on the soft spring grass, the film's charm crystallizes firm and makes solid its gay overwhelming appeal.

"*Funny Face* is the most original screen musical since *Seven Brides for Seven Brothers* and possibly the most enjoyable since *Singin' in the Rain*."

—John Cutts, *Films and Filming*

"It is reasonable to reckon that you won't see a prettier musical film—or one more extraordinarily stylish—during the balance of this year. If you do, you may count yourself fortunate, for this is a picture with class in every considerable department on which this sort of picture depends.

"It is a purely coincidental tale of a drab little Greenwich Village salesgirl who is grabbed by a pertinacious troupe of style-magazine super-worldlings, whisked off to Paris and turned into a dazzling superdress model, with whom the blasé photographer falls in love. But she can't stay out of those smoky cellars where the long-haired intellectuals live—not until one bearded cultist shows he's interested in more than her mind.

"Miss Hepburn has the meek charm of a wallflower turned into a rueful butterfly, and Mr. Astaire plays

110

FUNNY FACE   With Fred Astaire, performing "He Loves and She Loves"

FUNNY FACE With
Fred Astaire

FUNNY FACE Performing in the "Basal Metabolism" number

her lens-hound suitor softly, as if afraid to turn on too much steam. Even so, they make very nice music with such graceful Gershwin numbers as "He Loves and She Loves," "'S Wonderful" and the title song. Kay Thompson, the brittle cafe singer, is fantastic and funny as a style-magazine director."

—Bosley Crowther, *New York Times*

"Stanley Donen's *Funny Face* is perhaps the gayest and most invigorating musical since his own *Seven Brides for Seven Brothers*. The dance numbers are consistently inventive, and the film's rather sharp and consciously clever styling does not prevent it from achieving considerable charm. In spite of its extravagant settings, *Funny Face* is essentially an intimate musical and the three leading players effectively monopolise the screen. Fred Astaire plays with the im-

The "Basal Metabolism" number in *Funny Face*

mensely accomplished casualness that one expects, and is partnered in style by Audrey Hepburn, whose playing is both spirited and waif-like."

—"P. H.," *Monthly Film Bulletin*

"This big Stanley Donen musical isn't all it should be. You keep wanting it to turn into wonderful romantic fluff, but it's only spottily successful. The Leonard Gershe script is weak, particularly in Astaire's role, and the movie emphasizes Astaire's age by trying to ignore it. Still, Hepburn is a charming sidekick for Astaire, and the satirist Kay Thompson is agreeable as the rangy, hard-boiled fashion editor."

—Pauline Kael, *5001 Nights at the Movies*

"Hepburn not only looks her limpid best from first to last; she also does some snazzy dancing (she is better solo than Astaire), and even sings effectively in a sort of absinthetic *Sprechstimme* with a touch of wood alcohol in the low notes."

—*Time*

FUNNY FACE   With Fred Astaire, Michel Auclair, and Kay Thompson

Love in the Afternoon

LOVE IN THE AFTERNOON   As Ariane Chavasse

LOVE IN THE AFTERNOON   With Maurice Chevalier

CAST

Gary Cooper (*Frank Flanagan*); Audrey Hepburn (*Ariane Chavasse*); Maurice Chevalier (*Claude Chavasse*); John McGiver (*Monsieur X*); Van Doude (*Michel*); Lise Bourdin (*Madame X*); Bonifas (*Commissioner of Police*); Audrey Wilder (*Brunette at Opera*); Gyula Kokas, Michel Kokas, George Cocos, Victor Gazzoli (*The Four Gypsies*); Charles Bouillard (*Valet at the Ritz*); Olga Valery (*Lady With Dog*); Leila Croft and Valerie Croft (*Swedish Twins*); Andre Priez (*First Porter at the Ritz*); Gaidon (*Second Porter at the Ritz*); Minerva Pious (*Maid at the Ritz*); Filo (*Flanagan's Chauffeur*); Gregory Gromoff (*Doorman at the Ritz*); Janina Dard and Claude Ariel (*Existentialists*); Francois Moustache (*Butcher*); Gloria France (*Client at Butcher's*); Jean Sylvain (*Baker*); Annie Roudier (*First Client at Baker's*); Jeanne Charblay (*Second Client at Baker's*); Odette Charblay (*Third Client at Baker's*); Gilbert Constant and Monique Saintey (*Lovers on Left Bank*); Jacques Preboist and Anne Laurent (*Lovers Near the Seine*); Jacques Ary and Simone Vanlancker (*Lovers on Right Bank*); Richard Flagy (*Husband*); Jeanne Papir (*Wife*); Marcelle Broc and Marcelle Praince (*Rich Women*); Guy Delorme (*Gigolo*); Olivia Chevalier and Solon Smith (*Little Children in the Gardens*); Eve Marley and Jean Rieubon (*Tandemists*);

LOVE IN THE AFTERNOON   With John McGiver

LOVE IN THE AFTERNOON   With Gary Cooper

Christian Lude, Charles Lemontier, and Emile Mylos (*Generals*); Alexander Trauner (*Artist*); Betty Schneider, Charles Perrault, Vera Boccadoro, and Marc Aurian (*Couples Under Water Wagon*); Bernard Musson (*Undertaker*); Michele Selignac (*Widow*).

CREDITS

Producer-Director: Billy Wilder; *Assistant Director*: Paul Feyder; *Associate Producers*: William Schoor and Doane Harrison; *Screenwriters*: Billy Wilder and I. A. L. Diamond; *Based on the novel* Ariane *by* Claude Anet; *Cinematographer*: William Mellor; *Editor*: Leonid Azar; *Art Director*: Alexander Trauner; *Musical Adaptation*: Franz Waxman: *Musical Compositions*: "Fascination" by F. D. Marchetti and Maurice de Feraudy; "C'est Si Bon" by Henri Betti and Andre Hornez; "L'Ame des Poètes" by Charles Trenet; "Love in the Afternoon," "Ariane," and "Hot Paprika" by Matty Malneck; *Running time*: 130 minutes. Available on videocassette and laser disc.

ORIGINAL RELEASE

1957; an Allied Artists release of a Billy Wilder production.

THE FILM

Reunited with Billy Wilder, Audrey Hepburn once again found herself cast opposite a father figure in the person of Gary Cooper. Their vehicle was a Lubitsch-like comedy that derived from a Claude Anet novel called *Ariane*, and it had been filmed twice before, first in a 1931 German version (*Ariane*) with Elisabeth Bergner and Rudolf Forster, and a year later in a French edition (*Ariane, jeune fille russe*) that teamed Gaby Morlay and Victor Francen. Both adaptations clung to the novel's concept of an innocent young girl's winning over a middle-aged roué by feigning a romantic past of her own to equal his—and eventually reforming him altogether. In both of these versions, the actresses were actually in their midthirties, and their leading men a decade older. And so, while their eventual mating looked likely, critics conceded that the Misses Bergner and Morlay were straining credulity a bit as young virgins.

For *Ariane*'s third screen incarnation, however, producer-director Billy Wilder's choice of Hepburn for the girl made more sense. Wilder first sought Cary Grant (age fifty-two) for her costar, and then Yul

Brynner (forty-one), but neither was available. His third choice, Gary Cooper, looked old and tired beyond his fifty-five years, but it was decided that careful lighting and direction might solve the twenty-eight-year age discrepancy and enable audiences to accept their May-September romance. And, to a degree, audiences did, although more than one reviewer noted that Hepburn might have been better served had Cooper switched roles with the charming Maurice Chevalier, who played her father with a style and vitality that belied his sixty-eight years. Indeed, Hep-

burn and Chevalier evinced more on-screen chemistry than did Hepburn and Cooper.

Considering its slight plot, *Love in the Afternoon* (as *Ariane* was rechristened prior to release) runs far too long at 130 minutes. But Billy Wilder, in collaboration for the first time with his most successful coscreenwriter, I. A. L. Diamond, maintains an atmosphere of sly charm and amusing detail that *almost* sustains the film's length. And director Wilder is helped immeasurably by the luminous black-and-white photography of William Mellor and by musical

With Gary Cooper in *Love in the Afternoon* (1957)

LOVE IN THE AFTERNOON   With Gary Cooper and Lise Bourdin

adaptor Franz Waxman, whose various arrangements of the movie's long-playing leitmotif "Fascination" lend so much to the resulting effect.

CRITICS' CIRCLE

"'A comedy in the Lubitsch tradition,' Billy Wilder has said of *Love in the Afternoon*; and from this comment one could look forward to something frivolous, sophisticated and engaging. After all, Wilder had written some of Lubitsch's most amusing comedies (*Bluebeard's Eighth Wife*, *Ninotchka*, etc.) and his stylish cynicism promised to lend itself well to the film's story of an aging roué brought to heel by a young innocent. What finally emerges, however, is less of a Lubitsch confection than a Wilder concoction—wry, overlong, slightly uncertain in mood and only intermittently amusing. Some of the humor—particularly a magnificent quartet of gypsy musicians hired by the American (Gary Cooper) to provide 'mood' music for his amorous activities—strikes exactly the right note of light sophistication. The stylish performances of Audrey Hepburn and Maurice Chevalier are also in keeping. Only Cooper's tired and muffed playing tends to throw the balance off-centre; and without charm in this role, the final scenes can only appear a dubious ending."

—John Cutts, *Sight and Sound*

"What a charming lot of detail Mr. Wilder and Mr. Diamond have contrived to keep their unmoral story going for a couple of minutes over two hours! And what delightful performances Audrey Hepburn and Gary Cooper give as the cleverly calculating couple who spar through the amorous afternoons!"

—Bosley Crowther, *New York Times*

"It is cynical, amoral and highly artificial, and its whole ambience belongs to the Lubitsch era. The Ritz Hotel setting, the divorce detective, the gypsy band and champagne that make up Flanagan's apparatus of seduction, the film's carefully calculated transitions from cynicism to sentiment, are all part of a cinema tradition. A good deal of *Love in the Afternoon* lives up to it entertainingly; the dialogue, notably in the early scenes, is lightly and heartlessly witty, the direction entirely assured. But the film makes some notable errors of judgment: it surrenders to the fashion for

LOVE IN THE AFTERNOON   With Gary Cooper

LOVE IN THE AFTERNOON   With Gary Cooper

LOVE IN THE AFTERNOON   With Van Doude

LOVE IN THE AFTERNOON   With Maurice Chevalier

length, spinning out a slight little comedy situation over a couple of hours; and its conclusion, sentimentally treated as it is here, appears only tasteless. The film is entertainingly played by Audrey Hepburn, with another of her captivatingly wistful performances, and by Maurice Chevalier. But Gary Cooper's rich Ameri-

LOVE IN THE AFTERNOON   As Ariane Chavasse

119

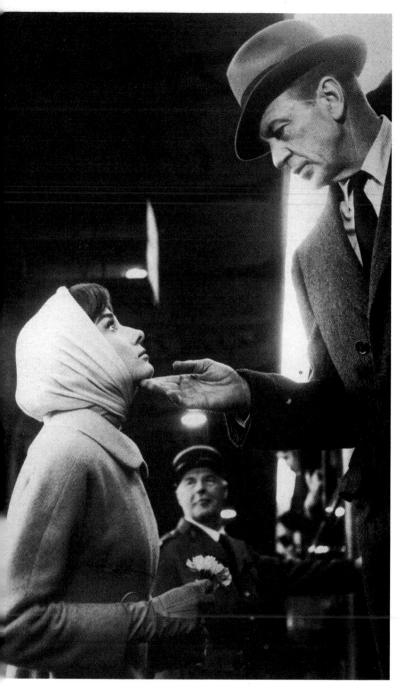

LOVE IN THE AFTERNOON   With Gary Cooper

can seems tired and middle-aged; and without the charm that Humphrey Bogart brought to a not dissimilar part in *Sabrina, Love in the Afternoon* itself looks jaded."

—"P. H.," *Monthly Film Bulletin*

"People who have been waiting since *Roman Holiday* for another good romantic comedy will be glad to hear that the long drought is over. *Love in the Afternoon* is a delightful film. It has that vague quality called charm, so often sought and so rarely achieved. It has sophisticated humor, and it may even bring an occasional tear to the eye. It is just a charade, a game played on the screen for fun, and Wilder sustains this spirit with dozens of small touches of the kind that we ordinarily admire in British comedies. And yet, if you believe in fairy tales—and there is nobody quite like Audrey Hepburn to make you believe—you will find that the outcome of this fable matters very much. You may not feel that it ends in the right way, but you will care. This is a tribute to Miss Hepburn, who is so winning in her youthful innocence and gaiety, so wistful when things go badly, that her impact on the jaded Cooper is easy to understand. Once again she will move her spectators to laugh and cry at almost the same time."

—William K. Zinsser, *New York Herald Tribune*

"It is all about romance before nightfall in Paris, with Audrey Hepburn and Gary Cooper as the participants. Under Billy Wilder's alternately sensitive, mirthful and loving-care direction, and with Maurice Chevalier turning in a captivating performance as a private detective specializing in cases of amour, the production holds enchantment and delight in substantial quantity."

—"Gene.," *Variety*

"I presume it is every man's privilege to fall in love with Audrey Hepburn. She is a tough girl to resist. At the moment, she is appearing in a delightful fantasy called *Love in the Afternoon*, and the object of her affection is Gary Cooper, portraying an aging American roué ensconced at the Paris Ritz. The story makes practically no sense, but it is airy and light, and really quite a treat."

—*New York Magazine*

"The allure of the movie depends almost entirely on the allure of these three institutionalized film personalities. After a time, even the most loyal fan is apt to wish for a change of face, of place and particularly of pace."

—*Newsweek*

Mayerling

With Mel Ferrer in *Mayerling* (1957)

CAST

Audrey Hepburn (*Maria Vetsera*); Mel Ferrer (*Prince Rudolf*); Raymond Massey (*Taafe, the Prime Minister*); Diana Wynyard (*The Empress*); Basil Sydney (*Emperor Franz Josef*); Judith Evelyn (*Countess Larische*); Isobel Elsom (*Baroness Vetsera*); Lorne Greene (*The Emperor's Aide*); Nancy Marchand (*Stephanie*); David Opatoshu and Nehemiah Persoff (*Police Officers*); and Ian Wolfe, John McGovern, Monique Van Vooren, Pippa Scott, and Michael Evans.

CREDITS

Director: Anatole Litvak; *Producers*: Anatole Litvak and Mort Abrahams; *Screenwriter*: Michael Dyne; *Based on the novel* Idyll's End *by* Claude Anet; *Sets*: Otis Riggs; *Costumes*: Dorothy Jeakins; *Musical Direction*: Georges Bassman; *TV running time*: 90 minutes.

ORIGINAL RELEASE

1957; an NBC-TV production for Producers' Showcase. (Released theatrically in Europe.)

THE FILM

Costarring for the first time since Broadway's *Ondine*, Audrey Hepburn and Mel Ferrer signed to make their joint "color TV debut" in NBC's Producers' Showcase presentation of *Mayerling*. Since its director-producer was Anatole Litvak, the man responsible for the 1936 Charles Boyer–Danielle Darrieux French classic of that title that had drawn international acclaim, the couple held high hopes for this project. Budgeted at a then-lavish $620,000, the ninety-minute "live" production boasted an impressive thirty sets and an elegant wardrobe, including ten costume changes for its leading lady. The drama was simultaneously recorded on film, since Hepburn's presence immediately meant a potential audience in Europe, where it was subsequently shown as a theatrical motion picture.

Mayerling derives from the true story of Austria's Crown Prince Rudolf and his teenage mistress Baroness Maria Vetsera, who died together under mysterious circumstances at his hunting lodge in the Vienna

MAYERLING With Mel Ferrer,
Raymond Massey, Diana Wynyard, and
Judith Evelyn

MAYERLING   With Raymond Massey, Diana Wynyard, Judith Evelyn, and Mel Ferrer

Woods in January 1889. Michael Dyne's script was based, like the 1936 movie, on Claude Anet's novel *Idyll's End*, and offers a logical solution to this real-life mystery that was never actually solved: that Rudolf—forced into a marriage of convenience by his father, Emperor Franz Josef—continued to meet with his true love, even flaunting his alliance with young Maria when they danced together at a palace ball. Eventually, Rudolf shoots his beloved and then commits suicide one night at the remote hunting lodge at Mayerling.

In 1949, Jean Marais and Doninique Blanchar portrayed the famed lovers in another French film, Jean Delannoy's *Le Secret de Mayerling* (The Secret of Mayerling), which posed a different ending that involved the couple's being assassinated by the prince's political enemies. The once-popular real-life mystery was filmed again in a 1958 Austrian version starring Rudolf Prack and Christiane Horbiger-Wessely, under the direction of Rudolf Jugert. Its most recent incarnation was the lavish 1968 French-British *Mayerling* with Catherine Deneuve and Omar Sharif as the glamorous pair, along with James Mason and Ava Gardner (as Sharif's mother!).

Undoubtedly, the television *Mayerling* attracted a great deal of attention, but many of the critics were less than kind, especially to Mel Ferrer. Although he and Hepburn would work together on future films, this was their last costarring project. Henceforth, Mel would team with other leading ladies, remaining behind the scenes on Audrey's movies. Whatever rapport they maintained in their private lives appeared lost upon stage or screen.

CRITICS' CIRCLE

"It was a spectacular on all counts except one, the drama. It was not hard to see where the money went. . . . But where was the story of *Mayerling*? It may be granted that the narrative is on the creaky side, that the account of the romantic crisis in the house of Habsburg has its full share of clichés. But in *Mayerling* there is the potential of a drama that still can move a viewer's feelings. Mr. Litvak's production was enacted with cold, almost clinical detachment.

"As the Archduke, Mr. Ferrer never really illuminated his role with any meaningful emotional intensity. There was not the warmth of true love finally discovered or the tragedy of its denial. Audrey Hep-

MAYERLING With Mel Ferrer

burn, as the young girl, was the proverbial vision in color video, but there was not that inner radiance and almost childlike adoration of the Archduke which makes *Mayerling* touch the heart."

—Jack Gould, *New York Times*

"Sharing the honors with Litvak was Miss Hepburn, for her vibrant and controlled love scenes and her unsophisticated youth captured the charm and compassion of this Viennese idyll. What could have been sentimental and maudlin was brought to life as a warm and feeling story. She was exquisite in her childlike beauty. Ferrer was the embodiment of soulful tragedy and if hardly the equal of Miss Hepburn in histrionics, this rates as one of his best performances to date."

—*Variety*

"The lovers seemed more fated to bore each other to death than to end their illicit alliance in a murder-suicide pact."

—Columnist Sheilah Graham

"Audrey Hepburn was called on to do little more than look beautiful and look smitten with maidenly adoration, an assignment which gave her no trouble at all."

—Jay Nelson Tuck, *New York Post*

123

Green Mansions

CAST

Audrey Hepburn (*Rima*); Anthony Perkins (*Abel*); Lee J. Cobb (*Nuflo*); Sessue Hayakawa (*Runi*); Henry Silva (*Kua-Ko*); Nehemiah Persoff (*Don Panta*); Michael Pate (*Priest*); Estelle Hemsley (*Cla-Cla*).

CREDITS

Director: Mel Ferrer; *Producer*: Edmund Grainger; *Screenwriter*: Dorothy Kingsley; *Based on the novel by* William Henry Hudson; *CinemaScope-Metrocolor Cinematographer*: Joseph Ruttenberg; *Editor*: Ferris Webster; *Art Directors*; William A. Horning and Preston Ames; *Set Decorators*: Henry Grace and Jerry Wunderlich; *Special Effects*: A. Arnold Gillespie, Lee LeBlanc, and Robert R. Hoag; *Costumes*: Dorothy Jeakins; *Music*: Bronislau Kaper; *Special Music*; Hector Villa-Lobos; *Title-Song Lyrics*: Paul Francis Webster; *Sung by* Anthony Perkins; *Marake Dance-Sequence Choreographer*: Katherine Dunham; *Running time*: 104 minutes. Available on videocassette.

ORIGINAL RELEASE

1959; a Metro-Goldwyn-Mayer Picture.

GREEN MANSIONS   With Anthony Perkins and Lee J. Cobb

GREEN MANSIONS   With Anthony Perkins

THE FILM

First published in Great Britain in 1904, W. H. Hudson's novel became a perennial bestseller, having been printed in almost every existing civilized language. In 1931, RKO first acquired rights to the book as a vehicle for first Dolores Del Rio, then Dorothy Jordan, and later Anne Shirley. But the project sat on a shelf until it was sold ten years later to an independent producer, James B. Cassidy. When he, in turn, failed to turn out a *Green Mansions* film, he sold rights in 1945 to Metro-Goldwyn-Mayer, who shelved plans for filming when casting and production appeared insurmountably difficult. In 1953, MGM signed Alan Jay Lerner to develop an adaptation, and they dispatched unit director William Kaplan and art director Preston Ames to South America to find suitable locations. At that time, *Green Mansions* actually went into production as a vehicle for that studio's Italian-born starlet Pier Angeli and Edmund Purdom, with Vincente Minnelli directing—but was soon abandoned, supposedly due to its star's pregnancy.

MGM screenwriter Dorothy Kingsley subsequently offered her adaptation to Mel Ferrer, who was seeking to package a showcase for his wife, with himself as her director. With MGM in agreement and Audrey Hepburn eager to work with her husband once again, Ferrer left for British Colombia, Guyana, and Venezuela to scout for locations. Eventually, *Green Mansions* became an amalgam of those exotic locales, blended with back-lot studio settings, where most of the dramatic action was filmed.

A viewing of the 1959 movie makes it understandable that *Green Mansions* proved a stumbling block for Hollywood producers; its filmy, romantic story of Rima, a "bird girl" of the South American rain forest who dwells with an old man claiming to be her grandfather (Lee J. Cobb), contained few of the surefire elements for a popular motion picture. The girl finds a sort of fleeting, platonic love with a young revolutionary named Abel (Anthony Perkins), who invades her domain in search of gold, but in the end Rima proves too delicate a creature to survive. After the old man dies, she's tracked down and burned in the forest treetops by superstitious Indians, who believe they are destroying an evil spirit. At the film's close, Abel appears to have found rapport with a miragelike vision of his late beloved. What might have proved acceptable for moviegoers of an earlier, simpler era could hardly have satisfied audiences of 1959. And certainly, the film's critics were not impressed.

CRITICS' CIRCLE

"In all fairness to MGM's lavish production of *Green Mansions*, I must admit that W. H. Hudson's lush romantic novel is almost impossible to reduce to film.

126

GREEN MANSIONS   With Anthony Perkins

His words invite the imagination—his forests have a quality of green never captured by Technicolor; Rima has an animal purity no actress could ever project. Let us say of this, then, that the camera has caught a quality of light that is often enchanting, that Audrey Hepburn's doe-like grace probably comes closer to a real-life Rima than we have any reason to expect, and that Mel Ferrer's direction manages to keep everything this side of Disneyland."

—Arthur Knight, *Saturday Review*

"Some four years of preparation have now produced what is virtually a female Tarzan story: a piece of irritating and often risible hokum with emphasis placed fatally on a considerably altered plot. Audrey Hepburn brings nothing relevant to the part of Rima but a faun-like appearance; she is too tense and camera-conscious, conveying anything but a feeling of communion with nature as she flits from tree to tree. Anthony Perkins as Abel suggests none of the

GREEN MANSIONS   With Anthony Perkins

With Anthony Perkins in
Green Mansions

With Lee J. Cobb in
Green Mansions (1959)

strength of character needed to make his trial of endurance with the Indians plausible, and only Henry Silva's powerful performance as the brave but ruthless Kua-Ko carries complete conviction."

—"D. B.," *Monthly Film Bulletin*

"This film version of the book catches little of the leafy rustle of Hudson's woodland fantasy. Audrey Hepburn is spritely enough, but actor Perkins clumps through the greenery as gingerly and gracelessly as an oversized boy scout bound for a merit badge in campcraft."

—*Newsweek*

"Some good location work is skillfully utilized, by process and editing, with backlot work. But Ferrer has been less successful in getting his characters to come alive, or in getting his audiences to care about them. Miss Hepburn is pretty as the strange young woman, but with no particular depth. Perkins seems rather frail for his role. Silva, on the other hand, gives an exciting performance, fatally damaging to Perkins, the hero, in their dramatic conflict."

—"Powe.," *Variety*

"The considerable talents of Miss Hepburn and Perkins seem curiously ineffective. Miss Hepburn's fragile beauty and delicate, perceptive face would

GREEN MANSIONS With Lee J. Cobb and Anthony Perkins

GREEN MANSIONS With
Lee J. Cobb and
Anthony Perkins

GREEN MANSIONS   With Lee J. Cobb

seem to fit her for this role, but in fact she seems curiously physical rather than elusive and insubstantial, which this heroine should be."

—Paul V. Beckley, *New York Herald Tribune*

"Without the ethereal Miss Hepburn vaporing lightly through the Venezuelan woods, floating out to charm a masculine intruder or poise wistfully with great tears in her eyes when she makes a sad discovery of man's deceptions, this could be a pretty foolish film. Even so, Miss Hepburn conducts herself all through it with grace and dignity, making Rima both poignant and idyllic, if not in the least logical. Obviously, she is not constructed to wear her thin garments sensually, so the poetry in the situation is not confused by bumptious sex."

—Bosley Crowther, *New York Times*

"Absurd studio-bound Shangri-La story based on an Edwardian fantasy that may well have suited the printed page, but not the wide screen. Dismally photographed in shades of green, with all concerned looking acutely uncomfortable."

—*Halliwell's Film Guide*

The Nun's Story

CAST

Audrey Hepburn (*Gabrielle Van der Mal/Sister Luke*); Peter Finch (*Dr. Fortunati*); Edith Evans (*Mother Emmanuel, Superior General*); Peggy Ashcroft (*Mother Mathilde*); Dean Jagger (*Dr. Van der Mal*); Mildred Dunnock (*Sister Margharita*); Beatrice Straight (*Mother Christophe*); Patricia Collinge (*Sister William*); Rosalie Crutchley (*Sister Eleanor*); Ruth White (*Mother Marcella*); Barbara O'Neil (*Mother Katherine*); Margaret Phillips (*Sister Pauline*); Patricia Bosworth (*Simone*); Colleen Dewhurst (*Archangel*); Stephen Murray (*Chaplain*); Lionel Jeffries (*Dr. Goovaerts*); Niall MacGinnis (*Father Vermeuhlen*); Eva Kotthaus (*Sister Marie*); Molly Urquhart (*Sister Augustine*); Dorothy Alison (*Sister Aurelie*); Jeanette Sterke (*Louise Van der Mal*); Errol John (*Illunga*); Diana Lambert (*Lisa*); Orlando Martins (*Kalulu*); Richard O'Sullivan (*Pierre Van der Mal*); Marina Wolkonsky (*Marie Van der Mal*); Penelope Horner (*Jeanette Milonet*); Ave Ninchi (*Sister Bernard*); Charles Lamb (*Pascin*); Ludovice Bonhomme (*Bishop*); Dara Gavin (*Sister Ellen*); Elfrida Simbari (*Sister Timothy*).

CREDITS

Director and Executive Producer: Fred Zinnemann; *Producer*: Henry Blanke; *Screenwriter*: Robert Ander-

THE NUN'S STORY   As Sister Luke

son; *Based on the novel by* Kathryn C. Hulme; *Technicolor Cinematographer*: Franz Planer; *Editor*: Walter Thompson; *Art Director*: Alexander Trauner; *Set Decorator*: Maurice Barnathan; *Music*: Franz Waxman:

THE NUN'S STORY   With Dean Jagger

Costumes: Marjorie Best; *Running time*: 149 minutes. Available on videocassette.

ORIGINAL RELEASE

1959; a Warner Brothers release of a Fred Zinnemann production.

THE FILM

Arguably, *The Nun's Story* may be the best motion picture that Audrey Hepburn ever made. And had it not been for her enthusiasm, it might not have been made at all. Producer-director Fred Zinnemann, who had read Kathryn C. Hulme's novel in galleys, found it difficult to interest any studio in financing the project—until Hepburn expressed interest in doing it. Until then, Hollywood thinking was best exemplified by one executive's question, "Who wants to see a documentary about how to become a nun?"

Indeed, the lengthy film's first part concentrates on the making of a nun as it follows Gabrielle Van der Mal, a young Belgian woman, from the time she takes leave of her saddened family to enter a strict Roman Catholic order, until her emergence as a full-fledged nursing nun, hopeful of following the medical vocation of her surgeon father. The story then shifts to the Congo, where Gabrielle—now known as Sister

THE NUN'S STORY   With Molly Urquhart, Eva Kotthaus, and Rosalie Crutchley

THE NUN'S STORY With Dean Jagger

Luke—serves under the guidance of the dedicated Dr. Fortunati (Peter Finch), an agnostic who takes pleasure in noting Sister Luke's minor infractions of her vows that would require confession. Finally, amid World War II, Sister Luke is back in Europe, serving in a Dutch hospital, where she learns of her father's death, shot by the Nazis while helping refugees to escape. It's an event of sufficient shock to make her question her faith, especially when she's refused permission to join the underground. For Sister Luke's long-suppressed struggle of inner conscience, this is the turning point; despite the counsel of her superiors, she decides, after seventeen long years of service (1927–44) to leave the order and return to the secular world to follow her headstrong beliefs.

As producer-director Zinnemann later wrote in *Focus on Film*, "This seems to me to be a universal theme. It applies to the—sometimes tragic—clash of an individual with the community of which he is a part; an individual who is trying to follow his own, personal conscience against all kinds of odds; it applies equally to a purely interior dilemma, where the conflict of conscience is not directed against an opponent, but rages within the soul of the individual himself."

THE NUN'S STORY With Colleen Dewhurst

Originally, Zinnemann had wanted *The Nun's Story* devoid of music, except for such Gregorian chants as might prove integral to the convent scenes. But Warners insisted on a full-fledged music score, and Franz Waxman's subsequent composition considerably enhances the movie. Zinnemann's sole musical "victory" involves the film's final sequence, in which Sister Luke is directed to a small room wherein she replaces her religious garb with lay clothing and is released without further human contact into a back alley connecting with a Belgian street. Waxman had originally written a triumphant theme for that scene, but Zinnemann successfully argued for silence, suggesting that Waxman's music might indicate that Warner Brothers was encouraging nuns to forsake their orders! And so *The Nun's Story* closes quietly and eloquently as the former Sister Luke, newly attired

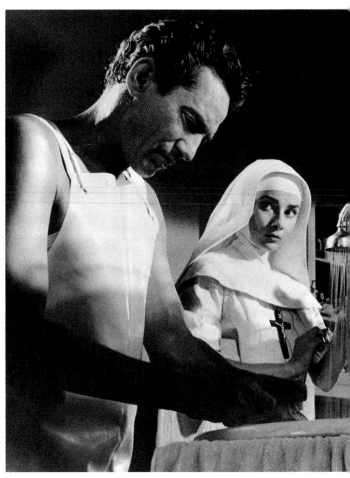

THE NUN'S STORY   With Peter Finch

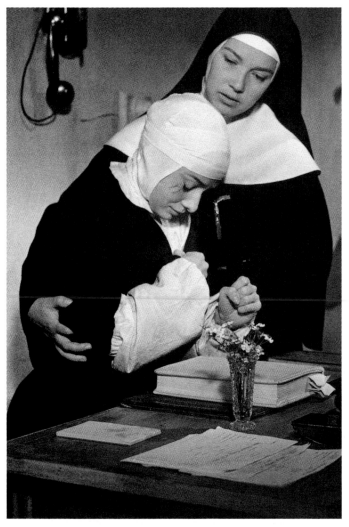

THE NUN'S STORY   With Dorothy Alison

for the outside world, turns her back on the convent and walks out into the daylight. The camera remains in the room she has just left as her figure recedes in the distance and "The End" silently appears on-screen. It has been said that *The Nun's Story* is the only instance of a Warner Brothers film *not* to have music over its end-title.

Before being edited to its release length of 149 minutes, *The Nun's Story* ran nearly four hours in its initial rough cut.

Zinnemann's tasteful handling of this subject matter, beautifully realized in Robert Anderson's adaptation and the performances of a dedicated cast (many in virtual cameo roles) resulted in considerable critical acclaim, as well as audience support. *The Nun's Story* garnered eight Academy Award nominations: Best Picture, nominations for Audrey Hepburn, Fred Zinnemann, and Robert Anderson, as well as for Franz Planer's color cinematography, Walter Thompson's film editing, Franz Waxman's score, and the picture's sound. But the movie failed to take home any Oscars; *Ben-Hur* won for Best Picture and Best Director William Wyler, and Simone Signoret took the Best Actress honors for *Room at the Top*. However, in the annual voting of the New York Film Critics, both Hepburn and Zinnemann emerged among 1959's winners, and the National Board of Review named *The Nun's Story* that year's Best Picture, and Fred Zinnemann its Best Director.

CRITICS' CIRCLE

"On the screen almost constantly is Audrey Hepburn in her mood of radiant, unspoken zeal that finds resources even when doubts and hazards grow hardest. On some of these occasions, she leaps into a momentary air of smug complacency, but this may have been deliberate to reveal that even this nun's nobility had its tiny crevices.

"In the convent sequences, Fred Zinnemann has directed his players almost as a pageant, often using mute processions and flashes of immobile faces to achieve his mood. Aside from the Congo doctor, crustily played by Peter Finch, only Miss Hepburn has a sustained role. No matter how great the supporting star, Zinnemann never allows an extra flourish of acting to call attention to the remarkable eminence and skill of these bit players. The subdued tone is seldom broken."

—Alton Cook, *New York World-Telegram*

"Fred Zinnemann's production is a soaring and luminous film. Audrey Hepburn has her most demanding film role, and she gives her finest performance. Despite the seriousness of the underlying theme, *The Nun's Story* has the elements of absorbing drama, pathos, humor, and a gallery of memorable scenes and characters.

"It is a long picture, and despite the necessity for careful preparation in the early scenes of the kind of life it is concerned with, some of the later scenes are drawn beyond their length. The ending, when it comes, seems abrupt and incomplete. Although the narrative reduces to fairly simple synopsis, it is a subtle and labyrinthine affair, and Robert Anderson's screenplay is exceptional in expressing the cerebral and spiritual conflict in vocal and pictorial terms. There is not a false note in it."

—"Powe.," *Variety*

THE NUN'S STORY   As Sister Luke

"The nun is played by Audrey Hepburn with such complete understanding of the full content of each scene that her performance will forever silence those who have thought her less an actress than a symbol of the sophisticated child-woman. In *The Nun's Story*, Miss Hepburn reveals the kind of acting talent that can project inner feelings of both depth and complexity so skillfully you must scrutinize her intently on a second and third viewing of the film to perceive how she does it. Her portrayal of Sister Luke is one of the great performances of the screen. So is Dame Edith Evans' as the Superior General. Dame Edith's face, her bearing, her voice and her movements are without flaw, and, even more important, they are imbued with the art that comes when, to perfected techniques and an emotional understanding of the role, there is added a player's own assent to the lines he must speak. Peter Finch has never played any role better than that of Dr. Fortunati. Finch's animal face and cerebral voice suggest the very dichotomy his role in *The Nun's Story* requires. The care Zinnemann exercised in casting even bit parts is only one of the directorial accomplishments he here displays."

—Henry Hart, *Films in Review*

"I couldn't be more respectful toward the accomplishment represented by *The Nun's Story*, a motion picture replete with skill, dignity, restraint and delicacy, and one that reflects enormous credit on Fred Zinnemann, who directed it, Robert Anderson, who wrote the screenplay, and Audrey Hepburn, who is the star.

"While there are moments of humor, terror and tragedy in this nun's tale, which keep it alive with interest, it is the more religious aspect that sets the film apart and makes it fascinating. This aspect has to do with the training and ritual that form so telling a part of the nun's special life, and for this the camera takes over and creates scenes of pictorial beauty. Motion picture becomes art, if only because one can't conceive a better instrument for otherwise evoking the impalpable appeal of this negation of worldliness. Franz Planer, one of the finest of Hollywood's craftsmen, was the photographer who, with Zinnemann, contributed to these striking, all but hypnotic sequences. . . .

"Miss Hepburn's face is often a mirror for the unspoken, but it is not quite enough (it can't all be done with acting and expression), nor are the episodes—among them the postulancy, her service in a hospital for the insane, her exhausting period of work in the Belgian Congo—very tightly knitted. Toward the close of the picture, the drama slows down.

THE NUN'S STORY With Peter Finch

136

THE NUN'S STORY   With Edith Evans

But at the end, when Sister Luke discards her vows and her habit and goes through that last symbolic door, the film once more gathers strength. Silence surrounds the spiritually tormented girl as she makes her solitary decision. Here all is admirable—Miss Hepburn's playing, and Mr. Zinnemann's impeccable taste."

—Hollis Alpert, *Saturday Review*

"The story is a true one, taken from a recent best-seller, but one feels that the film which Zinnemann envisaged when he first read the book has eluded him. Although Audrey Hepburn manages to convey some of the internal struggle of Sister Luke, she is unable to contain in her performance more than a fraction of what the part implies, since both direction

137

and script fail to dramatize this struggle. We are meant to understand that a battle is raging in the nun's soul, yet there are no scenes, no relationships, no incidents through which the conflict could be shown. The battery of distinguished actresses (Peggy Ashcroft, Mildred Dunnock, Patricia Collinge, Rosalie Crutchley) engaged to play nuns is wasted; they are given nothing to act, except for a series of monologues which might have been stolen straight from a book of convent rules. Only the parting between Dame Edith Evans, as the Mother Superior, and Miss Hepburn, when two people and not two mouthpieces confront each other, achieves some life. It is left to Peter Finch, in a short study of warm-hearted agnosticism, to bring a shock of genuine drama into the film."

—Kenneth Cavander, *Sight and Sound*

"To characterize this handsome picture as a conventional drama or romance or perhaps as an odd adventure story is a perilous thing to do, for it doesn't fit any category in an easy and obvious way. In a brilliant synthesis of idea and pictorial imagery, which includes stunning contrasts of color, the tempo of action and moods, Mr. Zinnemann has made this offbeat drama describe a parabola of spiritual afflatus and deflation that ends in a strange sort of defeat. For the evident point of this experience is that a woman gains but also loses her soul, spends and exhausts her devotion to an ideal she finds she cannot hold.

"In the role of the nun, Miss Hepburn is fluent and luminous. From her eyes and her eloquent expressions emerge a character that is warm and involved. A major musical score by Franz Waxman completes the artistry of this thoroughly tasteful film."

—Bosley Crowther, *New York Times*

"Audrey Hepburn plays with natural intelligence; Edith Evans, Peggy Ashcroft and Peter Finch fill comparatively small roles vividly. All things considered, *The Nun's Story* does show the degree of success possible with an exceptionally complex and adult theme executed in relatively conventional but fundamentally decent terms."

—"P. H.," *Monthly Film Bulletin*

"Turning a famous book into a film, Director Zinnemann makes *The Nun's Story* a hauntingly beautiful, tragic account of the battles that raged for seventeen years in one nun's soul. To help, he has a movie cast to perfection and a superb performance by Audrey Hepburn.

"The story, first told in Kathryn Hulme's book, is based on the experiences of Sister Luke, a Belgian girl who mistook a desire to nurse the sick for a religious vocation and joined a nursing order of nuns. She was a fine nurse, but after seventeen years of trying to be a good nun, she failed and was officially released from her vows. The film details her failures with compassion and wonder."

—*Life*

The Unforgiven

CAST

Burt Lancaster (*Ben Zachary*); Audrey Hepburn (*Rachel Zachary*); Audie Murphy (*Cash Zachary*); John Saxon (*Johnny Portugal*); Charles Bickford (*Zeb Rawlins*); Lillian Gish (*Mattilda Zachary*); Albert Salmi (*Charlie Rawlins*); Joseph Wiseman (*Abe Kelsey*); June Walker (*Hagar Rawlins*); Kipp Hamilton (*Georgia Rawlins*); Arnold Merritt (*Jude Rawlins*); Carlos Rivas (*Lost Bird*); Doug McClure (*Andy Zachary*).

CREDITS

Director: John Huston; *Producer*: James Hill; *Screenwriter*: Ben Maddow; *Based on the novel by* Alan Le May; *Panavision-Technicolor Cinematographer*: Franz Planer; *Editor*: Hugh Russell Lloyd; *Art Director*: Stephen Grimes; *Music*: Dimitri Tiomkin; *Costumes*: Dorothy Jeakins; *Special Effects*: Dave Koehler; *Running time*: 125 minutes. Available on videocassette.

ORIGINAL RELEASE

1960; a United Artists release of a coproduction of James Productions and Hecht-Hill-Lancaster.

THE UNFORGIVEN   As Rachel Zachary

THE FILM

In his autobiography, *An Open Book*, director John Huston called this film "a mistake." He had agreed to direct *The Unforgiven* not only on the basis of its Ben Maddow screenplay (adapted from a novel by Alan Le May, author of *The Searchers*), but also because of the strong cast already lined up by Hecht-Hill-Lancaster Productions: Burt Lancaster, Audrey Hepburn, Audie Murphy, Lillian Gish, and Charles Bickford among them. But Huston also sensed in the story's study of racial intolerance on the Texas frontier possibilities that had seldom been touched upon in

139

THE UNFORGIVEN   With June Walker, Charles Bickford, Lillian Gish, Audie Murphy, and Burt Lancaster

frontier times, and moviemaking dollars went further in Mexico, the production found more appropriate terrain in the surroundings of the old Mexican mining town of Durango, where, in an unfortunate accident, Audrey Hepburn was thrown from her white Arabian stallion, Gui Pago, and sustained a broken back. Pregnant at the time of the fall (a fact then unknown to the film's producers), she remained in bed for a month's rest, later requiring special back braces and careful treatment in order to complete the rugged production. In addition, Audie Murphy was nearly drowned in a freak duck-shooting accident with John

Hollywood Westerns. But as he explains it in his book, "The trouble was that the producers disagreed. What they wanted was what I had unfortunately signed on to make when I accepted the job in the first place—a swashbuckler about a larger-than-life frontiersman."

The film is set in the Texas Panhandle of the late 1860s, when the area's white settlers were often in bloody conflict with the Kiowa Indians. The story centers on the Zacharys, a ranch family consisting of the strong-willed matriarch Mattilda (Gish), her sons Ben (Lancaster), Cash (Murphy), and Andy (Doug McClure), and her adopted daughter, Rachel (Hepburn), whose full-blooded Kiowa origins are Mattilda's closely guarded secret. In a memorably creepy performance, Joseph Wiseman plays the film's catalyst, an itinerant, vengeful saddle tramp named Abe Kelsey, who spreads word of Rachel's roots among the Zacharys' less-than-tolerant neighbors, including the Rawlinses, whose son Charlie (Albert Salmi) Rachel appears destined to wed—until the Kiowa community, led by Rachel's charismatic blood-brother Lost Bird (Carlos Rivas), decides to get her back, at any cost. It all ends up in Indian attacks, much carnage, and a finale in which Hepburn and Lancaster appear bound for marriage and a rocky future in their racially biased land.

Because that part of Texas looked too modern for

Huston, and three of the movie's technicians were killed in a plane crash. With those attendant production delays and setbacks, *The Unforgiven* wound up costing in excess of $5 million, a sum not to be recouped by the picture's domestic box office, for it was less than a hit in the United States.

Following Audrey Hepburn's death, Lillian Gish stated, "In Mexico during the shooting, Audrey made me a gray wool poncho that I still wear every day during the winter. Now I'll never take it off."

THE UNFORGIVEN   With Lillian Gish

THE UNFORGIVEN   With John Saxon and Burt Lancaster

CRITICS' CIRCLE

"Alternating between moods of mystical brooding and crackling action, director John Huston has made a strange western in *The Unforgiven*. It casts a spell both fascinating and baffling.

"Burt Lancaster is a brawling bully as the head of

141

THE UNFORGIVEN   With June Walker

the clan beset by the rumored blood taint. There is raw strength as well as appealing delicacy in Audrey Hepburn's performance of the debated sister. She draws upon newly displayed resources for this remarkable portrayal.

"A dozen years ago, Huston made one of the greatest of all Westerns, *The Treasure of the Sierra Madre.* He has put the same masterful craft into *The Unforgiven.*"

—Alton Cook, *New York World-Telegram*

"Though it is almost twice the length, this first attempt by John Huston to design and execute a Western of heroic proportions arouses, curiously enough, much the same vague feelings of dissatisfaction as his studio-mutilated *Red Badge of Courage*; and, intermittently, much the same admiration. The visual style, aided by Franz Planer's photography with its stark tableaux, brooding night sequences and bird's-eye exteriors, is impressive. Huston's gifts as a storyteller are surprisingly muted; characters such as the half-breed Johnny Portugal appear and equally abruptly disappear; entire sequences lack the support of either character or resolution. Apart from Lillian

THE UNFORGIVEN   With Charles Bickford and Lillian Gish

THE UNFORGIVEN   With Burt Lancaster, Doug McClure, Audie Murphy, and Lillian Gish

THE UNFORGIVEN   With Doug McClure and Burt Lancaster

Gish and Doug McClure, none of the performances is exactly satisfactory."

—Peter John Dyer, *Monthly Film Bulletin*

"As the girl, Audrey Hepburn is a bit too polished, too fragile and civilized among such tough and stubborn types as Burt Lancaster as the man of the family, Lillian Gish as the thin-lipped frontier mother and Audie Murphy as a redskin-hating son.

"The scenery is great, the horses vigorous. Those who expect to see a settlement of the racial question will not be satisfied."

—Bosley Crowther, *New York Times*

THE UNFORGIVEN   With Doug McClure

As Rachel Zachary in *The Unforgiven*

"Miss Hepburn gives a shining performance as the foundling daughter of a frontier family. As her foster brother, obviously desperately in love with his 'sister,' Lancaster is fine as the strong-willed, heroic family spokesman and community leader. Miss Gish is okay as the mother; however, she has a tendency to over-react emotionally. Audie Murphy is surprisingly good as Lancaster's hot-headed brother whose hatred of Indians causes him to abandon his family. Dimitri Tiomkin's music tends to telegraph the action."

—"Holl.," *Variety*

"In the novel, the character Miss Hepburn plays was a white girl. The changes Ben Maddow made in the novel, to be credible, require still other changes of plot and characterization, which Maddow did not make. Put it down to Miss Hepburn's charm, and acting ability, that Maddow's ideational confusion didn't completely ruin this picture. Miss Hepburn does not save *The Unforgiven* all by herself. Franz Planer's beautiful Panavision photography of noble scenery is the film's greatest asset, and there are also good performances by Charles Bickford, Lillian Gish, Joseph Wiseman and John Saxon (whose part, but for a fragment, was edited out). *The Unforgiven* isn't an important picture, but it's the best Huston has directed in some time."

—Albert "Hap" Turner, *Films in Review*

THE UNFORGIVEN With
Burt Lancaster

"*The Unforgiven* may have its faults, but a great many of its sequences are, in my opinion, vintage Huston. Atmospherically, it is near-perfect, and in spite of some tendency to slow development, it has great excitement, and at climactic moments, as when Miss Gish hangs her tormentor, it rises to heights of savage drama. It is not a picture to be missed.

"As for Miss Hepburn, it is not her finest role; she doesn't really seem indigenous to the country or the people in spite of the fact an effort has been made to give her a look of buckskin roughness."

—Paul V. Beckley, *New York Herald Tribune*

With Audie Murphy in *The Unforgiven* (1960)

Breakfast at Tiffany's

CAST

Audrey Hepburn (*Holly Golightly*); George Peppard (*Paul Varjak*); Patricia Neal ("*2E*"); Mickey Rooney (*Mr. Yunioshi*); Buddy Ebsen (*Doc Golightly*); Martin Balsam (*O. J. Berman*); Jose-Luis de Villalonga (*Jose da Silva Perreira*); Dorothy Whitney (*Mag Wildwood*); Alan Reed (*Sally Tomato*); John McGiver (*Tiffany Salesman*); Stanley Adams (*Rusty Trawler*); Beverly Hills (*Nightclub Dancer*); Claude Stroud (*Sid Arbuck*); Elvia Allman (*Librarian*); Michael Quinn (*Man with Eye Patch*); Gil Lamb (*Party Guest*).

CREDITS

Director: Blake Edwards; *Producers*: Martin Jurow and Richard Shepherd; *Screenwriter*: George Axelrod; *Based on the novella by* Truman Capote; *Technicolor Cinematographer*: Franz F. Planer; *Editor*: Howard Smith; *Art Directors*: Hal Pereira and Roland Anderson; *Set Decorators*: Sam Comer and Ray Moyer; *Music*: Henry Mancini; *Song*: "Moon River" *by* Henry Mancini and Johnny Mercer, *sung by* Audrey Hepburn; *Special Effects*: John P. Fulton; *Costume Supervisor*: Edith Head; *Miss Hepburn's Wardrobe*: Hubert de Givenchy; *Miss Neal's Wardrobe*: Pauline Trigere; *Running time*: 115 minutes. Available on videocassette and laser disc.

ORIGINAL RELEASE

1961; a Paramount release of a Jurow–Shepherd production.

THE FILM

Without a doubt, *Breakfast at Tiffany's*—and its eternally haunting Henry Mancini–Johnny Mercer theme song, "Moon River"— will continue to be among the things for which Audrey Hepburn is most fondly remembered, for the role of Holly Golightly— adorable kook and Manhattan party girl, who lives by her wits and depends on the indulgences of men—is one she made very much her own. It's difficult to imagine anyone else as Holly, despite the fact that Holly's creator, novelist Truman Capote (who reputedly based her on his friend Doris Lilly) is said to have wanted Marilyn Monroe to portray her on-screen. Hepburn made Holly so endearing a singular creation that subsequent attempts to portray the character (Mary Tyler Moore in David Merrick's disastrous 1966 Broadway flop musical, *Breakfast at Tiffany's* which closed in previews; Stefanie Powers in the never-aired 1969–70 ABC-TV season pilot called *Holly Golightly*) were soon forgotten. Now, some thirty-odd years after its initial release, Paramount has seen fit to issue a letter-boxed edition of the 1961 *Breakfast at Tiffany's* in a high-priced "collectors' edition," sound proof that this motion picture has stood the test of time.

Breakfast at Tiffany's was originally a short novel, published in 1958, along with three other Truman Capote stories, in a form that resembled Christopher Isherwood's *Berlin Stories*, about Sally Bowles, the wacky, amoral heroine of 1930s Berlin. In both tales, the author creates for his heroine a platonic male friend and sounding board who represents himself.

And in each case, the literary work enjoyed a dramatic adaptation in which its male protagonist enjoyed a romantic relationship with the lady. In Capote's novella, salty-tongued "Miss Holiday Golightly" is last heard from in South America, where she (hopefully) has found (or will find) love and financial stability of some sort. On film, however, she winds up with the "kept boy" (George Peppard), a fellow tenant in her fashionably situated Manhattan building, courtesy of a wealthy married woman (Patricia Neal), who is explained away as his "decorator." As adapted for the screen by George Axelrod and directed by Blake Edwards, *Breakfast at Tiffany's* retains relatively little of the Capote creation, but it remains a delightful New York fairy tale of charming ne'er-do-wells who eventually find strength in one another and end up seemingly bound for honest and respectable futures in the company of the nameless ginger-colored cat who symbolizes their own needy rootlessness.

BREAKFAST AT TIFFANY'S   Holly at Tiffany's

With George Peppard and Patricia Neal in *Breakfast at Tiffany's*

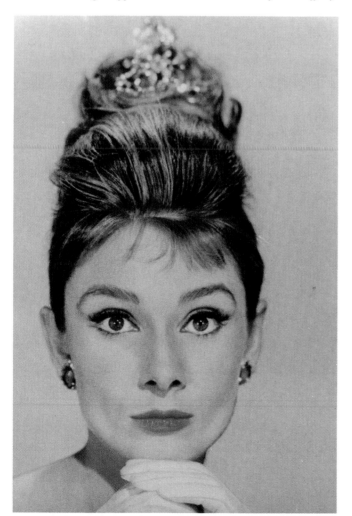

At Academy Award time, *Breakfast at Tiffany's* racked up nominations for Audrey Hepburn, Axelrod's screenplay, and the film's art direction/set decoration, while winning statuettes for "Moon River" as Best Song and for Henry Mancini's score. Beating out Audrey for that year's Best Actress Oscar was Sophia Loren in the Italian-made *Two Women*, the first and to date only actress to win for a foreign-language performance.

In a 1990 interview, Hepburn allowed as how "we couldn't have kept all the lines of the book; the censors wouldn't have allowed it. Besides, I don't think that Holly really has known as many men as she pretends. It's just a jazzy facade she creates, because basically she's a small-town girl who's out of her depth."

Breakfast at Tiffany's was originally to have been directed by John Frankenheimer, a New York television veteran whose feature debut had been 1957's low-budget *The Young Stranger*. In fact, he and screenwriter George Axelrod had already spent some time working on the script when, according to Frankenheimer, "Audrey Hepburn was cast in the picture

As Holly Golightly in *Breakfast at Tiffany's* (1961)

and I was fired, because, of course, she had never heard of me. I had directed a lot of television but only one film—so I was canned." Replacing Frankenheimer, whose forte was drama, marked a major breakthrough for Blake Edwards, with seven lighthearted movies to his credit, chief among them the Cary Grant–Tony Curtis comedy, *Operation Petticoat*.

Equally important to Hepburn among the assets of *Breakfast at Tiffany's* was its "Moon River" theme song, whose plaintive strains are heard at the movie's outset as a taxi deposits Holly Golightly at the doors of that exclusive Fifth Avenue emporium by dawn's early light. As its composer, Henry Mancini, recalled in a collection of posthumous tributes to Hepburn, "'Moon River' was written for her. No one else had ever understood it so completely. There have been more than a thousand versions of 'Moon River,' but hers is unquestionably the greatest. When we previewed the film, the head of Paramount was there, and he said, 'One thing's for sure. That f——g song's gotta' go.' Audrey shot right up out of her chair! Mel Ferrer had to put his hand on her arm to restrain

BREAKFAST AT TIFFANY'S   With "Cat"

With George Peppard in *Breakfast at Tiffany's*

her. That's the closest I have ever seen her come to losing control."

According to yet another source, the star's rejoinder to that ill-advised executive order was, "Over my dead body!"

CRITICS' CIRCLE

"The film's major delight comes from the inspired, off-beat casting of Audrey Hepburn as Capote's amoral, vanilla-haired Holly Golightly. Whether demanding

BREAKFAST AT TIFFANY'S   With George Peppard

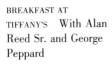

BREAKFAST AT TIFFANY'S   With Alan Reed Sr. and George Peppard

150

powder-room money from a gentleman escort, sipping a drink in the most hilarious cocktail party ever put on the screen, or taking a Crackerjack ring to Tiffany's for engraving, she creates an aura of belief without which the film would immediately disintegrate. Let others worry whether a love affair between a kept man and a call girl can—or should—end happily. Let those who are so minded object to the film's contrived and too-pat ending and then consider what Capote's own implied finale would have looked like on the screen. Blake Edwards and his talented crew have touched a tawdry romance with true glamour, and they held me unprotesting in that glamour world for two delightful hours."

—Arthur Knight, *Saturday Review*

"Blake Edwards's *Breakfast at Tiffany's*, glowingly adapted by George Axelrod from Truman Capote's

BREAKFAST AT TIFFANY'S   With "Cat"

BREAKFAST AT TIFFANY'S   With George Peppard

BREAKFAST AT TIFFANY'S   Singing "Moon River"

151

BREAKFAST AT TIFFANY'S Long ago, when Holly was still known as Ulamae, with Buddy Ebsen (*in hat*)

far more acerbic story, is about a ravishing, scared girl called Holly Golightly who reserves for jewels and money the steady passion that most girls feel only for a man when they are in love. The achievement of the film, as well as its hedging flaw, is that one leaves this unquestioned at the time. *Breakfast at Tiffany's* is a fable that silences carping, acted in a mood of guileless sympathy with the characters' quirks. It is only afterwards that the pea under the mattress begins to bore into one's bones.

"The happy ending of the film is as true to its scampering spirits as Capote's fade-out was true to his own much more stinging original. The speciousness lies in sweetening the character of the heroine so that she can be played by Audrey Hepburn without in any way changing her motives or actions, which remain monstrously avaricious. Truman Capote noticed, for instance, that her eyes sometimes had 'an assessing squint like a jeweler's,' that she could wear 'a tough, tiny smile that advanced her age immeasurably,' and that she was capable of vague-seeming well-placed bitchery. The book observes the streak of cold brutality that is often present in the romantic; the film merely sees the vivacity and sweetness of Audrey Hepburn."

—Penelope Gilliatt, *New Yorker*

BREAKFAST AT TIFFANY'S With Buddy Ebsen and George Peppard

"Audrey Hepburn may not be your (or Truman Capote's) notion of the amoral and pixyish Holly Go-lightly, but she's still enchanting enough to make *Breakfast at Tiffany's* worth watching. George Peppard and a sleek Henry Mancini score lend fine support; and, during repeated viewings, you might take special pleasure in Martin Balsam's portrait of a brash Hollywood agent and Patricia Neal's sophisticated lady. Mickey Rooney's Japanese photographer is a bit much—and so is the slick Hollywood happy ending to Holly's story. But Miss Hepburn is so charming that the brief bog-downs are easily forgiven."

—Judith Crist, *TV Guide*

"There is a real zest in the crotchety, wistful, hare-brained, lovely creature played by Audrey Hepburn. For me, the film's peak was reached with the cocktail party in which a dossier of kooks ran through their tricks with a kind of inane glee, but not only was this sequence never topped, the whole picture thereafter slid higgedly-piggedly downhill into a puddle of lemon meringue.

"Capote's Holly was harder, but I suppose hard girls aren't very popular, so Miss Hepburn's Holly is

BREAKFAST AT TIFFANY'S With George Peppard

BREAKFAST AT TIFFANY'S   Holly comes to terms with her future

Capote buffs may find some of Axelrod's fanciful alterations a bit too precious, pat and glossy for comfort, but enough of the original's charm and vigor have been retained to make up for the liberties taken with character to erect a marketable plot. What makes *Tiffany's* an appealing tale is its heroine, Holly Golightly, a charming, wild and amoral 'free spirit' with a latent romantic streak. Axelrod's once-over-go-lightly erases the amorality and bloats the romanticism, but retains the essential spirit of the character, and, in the exciting person of Miss Hepburn, she comes vividly to life on the screen, complemented by the reserved, capable work of George Peppard. Cinematically, the film is a sleek, artistic piece of craftsmanship."

—"Tube.," *Variety*

"A completely unbelievable but wholly captivating flight into fancy. Above all, it has the overpowering attribute known as Audrey Hepburn, who, despite her normal, startled-faun exterior, now is displaying a fey, comic talent that should enchant Truman Capote, who created the amoral pixie she portrays, as well as moviegoers meeting her for the first time. All the quick-silverish explanations still leave the character as implausible as ever. But in the person of Miss Hepburn, she is a genuinely charming, elfin waif who will be believed and adored."

—A. H. Weiler, *New York Times*

pert, bright in a fragile crystalline sort of way, but she isn't hard and it makes what the film keeps saying about her quite impossible to believe. Peppard doesn't seem to be entirely comfortable. Buddy Ebsen turns in a good performance as Miss Hepburn's former husband from Texas. Martin Balsam's Hollywood agent, who is acute enough to recognize that if Miss Hepburn's Holly is a phony, she's a 'real' phony because she believes it, has one of the more consistent characterizations and makes the most of it.

"What started with a sort of wiry blend of satire and pathos is finally allowed to dissolve into a kind of quack nostrum, only hopefully romantic, only limply comic."

—Paul V. Beckley, *New York Herald Tribune*

"Whitewashed and solidified for the screen, Truman Capote's *Breakfast at Tiffany's* emerges an unconventional, but dynamic entertainment that will be talked about. Out of the elusive, but curiously intoxicating Capote fiction, scenarist George Axelrod has developed a surprisingly moving film, touched up into a stunningly visual motion picture experience.

BREAKFAST AT TIFFANY'S   With George Peppard and "Cat"

The Children's Hour

(THE LOUDEST WHISPER)

THE CHILDREN'S HOUR   As Karen Wright

CAST
Audrey Hepburn (*Karen Wright*); Shirley MacLaine (*Martha Dobie*); James Garner (*Dr. Joe Cardin*); Miriam Hopkins (*Mrs. Lily Mortar*); Fay Bainter (*Mrs. Amelia Tilford*); Karen Balkin (*Mary Tilford*); Veronica Cartwright (*Rosalie Wells*); Jered Barclay (*Grocery Boy*); and (cut from release print) Carl Benton Reid (*Judge Potter*).

CREDITS
Producer-Director: William Wyler; *Associate Producer*: Robert Wyler; *Screenwriter*: John Michael Hayes; *Adapted from her play by* Lillian Hellman; *Cinematographer*: Franz F. Planer; *Editor*: Robert Swink; *Art Director*: Fernando Carrere; *Set Decorator*: Edward G. Boyle; *Music*: Alex North; *Costumes*: Dorothy Jeakins; *Running time*: 107 minutes. Available on videocassette.

ORIGINAL RELEASE
1962; a United Artists release of a Mirisch production.

THE FILM
Lillian Hellman based her debut play—a strong and well-received psychodrama about two schoolteachers whose lives are destroyed by a malicious child's lie—on a Scottish court case of the early nineteenth century. Anne Revere and Katherine Emery starred in the play that chalked up a successful 691-performance run during the 1934–35 Broadway season. The play also remains a landmark in that its failure to win that season's Pulitzer Prize for drama (Zoë Akins's sentimental sudser *The Old Maid* undeservedly took that honor) resulted in New York's outraged press members organizing themselves as the Drama Critics Circle, in order to give their own prize to each year's best play.

THE CHILDREN'S
HOUR   With James
Garner, Fay Bainter, and
Shirley MacLaine

THE CHILDREN'S
HOUR   With Veronica
Cartwright, Fay Bainter,
and Karen Balkin

THE CHILDREN'S HOUR   With James Garner and Shirley MacLaine in a scene cut from the release print

Film producer Samuel Goldwyn defied the Production Code advisers who tried to discourage his bringing *The Children's Hour* to the screen. In fact, he was even forbidden to use that then-notorious title (he called his 1936 adaptation *These Three*). Nor was he allowed to even suggest that lesbianism was a part of the story's theme. This Goldwyn solved, with the aid of Hellman's own adaptation of her stage work,

by having the child's lie suggest a man-woman sexual liaison carried on in the girls' school, rather than an all-female one between the teachers. Since the theme of the power of a lie remained valid, *These Three* is an excellent film that still holds a lot of strength, due to William Wyler's tight direction of a good cast (Merle Oberon, Miriam Hopkins, Joel McCrea, and Bonita Granville among them), all doing some of their very best work for a demanding taskmaster.

When Wyler's 1962 remake was being planned —in an era that could finally deal with the lesbian theme and the title *The Children's Hour*—he tried to lure his 1936 stars, Oberon and Hopkins, back, this

THE CHILDREN'S HOUR   With Shirley MacLaine

THE CHILDREN'S HOUR   With Shirley McLaine

time in the respective roles of the child's wealthy grandmother and the frivolous-actress aunt of one of the teachers. Hopkins wisely agreed, since her best screen performances had frequently been in Wyler films, but Oberon (still beautiful and glamorous at fifty) couldn't face the idea of portraying her own age, and deferred to sixty-nine-year-old Fay Bainter, whose Academy Award nomination attests to her wonderfully expressive acting.

As the two young women, former classmates who have managed to establish a small but successful school for young girls, Audrey Hepburn and Shirley MacLaine were called upon to portray emotions unlike any they had approached before. Apparently, during production there was pressure from the film's distributor, United Artists, to downplay the lesbian aspects of the story. Shirley MacLaine has since spoken of her frustrations when Wyler made her tone down her interpretation by eliminating brief scenes that would help establish what she was working so hard to characterize. And yet her facial reactions and line readings, in scenes with Hepburn's visiting suitor, James Garner, continue to make marks for a fine performer's intelligent choices. Also eliminated from the release print of *The Children's Hour* was a climactic courtroom sequence showing why and how the two teachers lose their libel suit against the child and her grandmother who have maligned them, causing all the other parents to withdraw their children from the school.

But despite its various excellences, *The Children's Hour* was little appreciated in 1962, and most of the movie's reviewers found one thing or another to carp

THE CHILDREN'S HOUR   With Fay Bainter

THE CHILDREN'S HOUR   With James Garner

most unpretty suicide. Using his camera as scalpel, Franz Planer probes with surgical precision. Wyler, a master craftsman, retains a subtle, genuine compassion for the women without detracting from the harshness of their dilemma. Miss Hepburn's frail beauty belies the emotional power with which she projects strength. Miss MacLaine displays integrity in her role as a deviate and never veers one degree off course. James Garner, ploddingly coming of age as an actor, plays with restraint. Fay Bainter is magnificent as the woman who engineers the spread of slander, and Miriam Hopkins as an insolvent, troublemaking aunt plays with utter conviction."

—Show Business Illustrated

"It is hard to believe that Lillian Hellman's famous stage play could have aged into such a cultural antique in the course of three decades as it looks in this new film version. It is incredible that educated people living in an urban American community today would react as violently and cruelly to a questionable innuendo as they are made to do in this film. So this

about. It remains an underrated film whose most negative aspect is the unfortunate casting of the young catalyst, twelve-year-old Mary Tilford. A far cry from the wonderfully bratty performance of Bonita Granville in the 1936 version, young Karen Balkin's blatant grimacing and overemphasized speech patterns are so obnoxious that one can only lament the uncharacteristic failure of William Wyler to curb her excesses and get a decent performance out of her.

In addition to Bainter's well-deserved Oscar nomination, there were others for Franz F. Planer's black-and-white cinematography, as well as the picture's art direction, sound, and costume design, with Audrey Hepburn relinquishing her beloved Givenchy to accept the suitably less chic wardrobe created by Dorothy Jeakins, with whom she'd worked on *Green Mansions* and *The Unforgiven*.

CRITICS' CIRCLE

"Gaining a dreadful momentum, the drama builds slowly, inexorably, to Miss MacLaine's acknowledgment that a lie has found her out and, finally, to her

THE CHILDREN'S HOUR   Karen discovers Martha's body

159

drama that was supposed to be so novel and daring because of its muted theme is really quite unrealistic and scandalous in a prim and priggish way. What's more, it is not too well acted, except by Audrey Hepburn. She gives the impression of being sensitive and pure. Shirley MacLaine inclines to be too kittenish in some scenes and to do too much vocal hand-wringing toward the end.

—Bosley Crowther, *New York Times*

"Honesty and good taste are abundantly present in this new version of *The Children's Hour*. But the entire film seems curiously dated, as if all the characters had been strangely insulated against any knowledge of modern psychology. On the other hand, in terms of sheer moviemaking, William Wyler again proves himself the master of the cinematized stage play. Whether his camera is still or roving, it invariably matches the pace and tension of the scene being played before it. The precision of his shot-to-shot relationships is unexcelled by any other director. He is still inventive in the creation of cinematic effects, as in the sense of panic he evokes with a rapid series of shots of Audrey Hepburn racing across a lawn to the locked room of Shirley MacLaine. Always a perfectionist, he obtains top performances from every one of his principals (although in the interest of verisimilitude, Hepburn and MacLaine might well have switched roles)."

—Arthur Knight, *Saturday Review*

"Somewhat dated, but a bold, brisk and faithful remake of Lillian Hellman's play. If there is a fault to be found with the new version, it is that the sophistication of modern society makes the events in Miss Hellman's play slightly less plausible in the 1961 setting into which it has been framed. But this is a minor reservation overshadowed by the general excellence of Wyler's production and the durable power

of the playwright's work. The personalities of Audrey Hepburn and Shirley MacLaine beautifully complement each other. Miss Hepburn's soft sensitivity, marvelous projection and emotional understatement result in a memorable portrayal. Miss MacLaine's enactment is almost equally rich in depth and substance."

—"Tube.," *Variety*

"Shirley MacLaine, all forlorn, gives the best performance of her career as the teacher who is sickened to find that she is partly homosexual. She gives viewers a touching and indelible lesson in what cinema acting is all about. But Audrey Hepburn gives her standard, frail, indomitable characterization, which is to say that her eyes water constantly (frailty) and her chin is forever cantilevered forward (indomitability). Little is asked of James Garner, and he gives it. Wyler's notion of registering childish malevolence is to have twelve-year-old actress Balkin roll her eyes, scowl, bare her teeth and jerk her head back like a duchess regarding a spider, every time she is on camera."

—*Time*

"What makes Miss MacLaine's performance so much more trenchant is that while Miss Hepburn is asked to portray little more than disbelief, defiance and the posture of pride, Miss MacLaine is absolutely involved. Her scene of horrible and fatal self-reproach is the most affecting psychological event in the picture and its dramatic high point. It is only in this one instant that the false accusation theme and the implied theme of lesbian love suddenly coincide, and the action, though internal, becomes immediate, actual and striking."

—Paul V. Beckley, *New York Herald Tribune*

Charade

CAST

Cary Grant (*Peter Joshua*); Audrey Hepburn (*Reggie Lambert*); Walter Matthau (*Hamilton Bartholomew*); James Coburn (*Tex Penthollow*); George Kennedy (*Herman Scobie*); Ned Glass (*Leopold Gideon*); Jacques Marin (*Inspector Grandpierre*); Paul Bonifas (*Felix*); Dominique Minot (*Sylvie Gaudet*); Thomas Chelimsky (*Jean-Louis Gaudet*).

CREDITS

Producer-Director: Stanley Donen; *Associate Producer*: James Ware; *Screenwriters*: Peter Stone and Marc Behm; *Technicolor Cinematographer*: Charles Lang Jr.; *Editor*: James Clark; *Art Director*: Jean D'Eaubonne; *Music*: Henry Mancini; *Title Song by* Henry Mancini and Johnny Mercer; *Miss Hepburn's Wardrobe*: Hubert de Givenchy; *Running time*: 113 minutes. Available on videocassette.

ORIGINAL RELEASE

1963; a Universal Pictures release of a Stanley Donen production.

THE FILM

Charade returned Audrey Hepburn to the company

As Regina Lambert in *Charade*

of yet another of Hollywood's senior superstars, this time Cary Grant, whose earlier "unavailability" for *Sabrina* matched her with Humphrey Bogart. Initially, Grant was concerned about the age difference between himself and his *Charade* teammate—until screenwriter Peter Stone put him at ease with the addition of dialogue that made light of their apparent disparity in years. Physical romantic scenes were wisely kept to a minimum, allowing the on-screen Grant-Hepburn relationship to emanate largely from their natural chemistry and the imagination of their audiences. In a late-1963 *Look* interview, Grant commented, "All I want for Christmas is another movie

CHARADE   As Regina Lambert

suddenly widowed (and about to be divorced) young woman who finds herself the target of a gang of predatory men. Charles Lang Jr.'s Technicolor photography and an inspired and infectious score by Henry Mancini complete the magic, and there's an amusingly 007-style beginning to the film as Mancini's clangy, intentionally derivative theme music accompanies the rapid-fire opening titles of Maurice Binder, who created the Bond film titles in similar fashion. A body thrown from a moving train quickly sets the tone for action and suspense, shifting to a mountain ski resort, where the close-up of a gun pointed at Audrey Hepburn reveals the weapon to be a child's water pistol, informing us that at least part of the ensuing melodrama will be tongue-in-cheek.

With its cunning blend of box-office stars, good writing, expert direction, and engaging settings, *Charade* could hardly miss. And what the movie lacks in

with Audrey Hepburn!" Indeed, he tried to get her for the following year's *Father Goose*, but had to settle for Leslie Caron when Hepburn's commitments interfered. In turn, Warner Brothers wanted Grant for Hepburn's *My Fair Lady* costar, reasoning that Broadway's Rex Harrison had passed his prime as a movie attraction; Grant not only turned Jack Warner down but insisted that Harrison was the only man to portray the film Henry Higgins. Their final opportunity to reunite professionally came when MGM unsuccessfully tried to lure Grant out of retirement with its semimusical 1969 remake of *Goodbye, Mr. Chips*, for which it also hoped to engage Hepburn. Metro finally went with Peter O'Toole and Petula Clark.

Fortunately, filmgoers have the lighthearted Hitchcock-like intrigues of *Charade* to cherish. It was produced and directed to perfection by Stanley Donen (*Funny Face*), who made good use of his Parisian and Alpine locations to recount this complex tale of a

162

narrative smoothness and believability is more than compensated for in style and wit. *Charade* was among Universal's more successful 1963 motion pictures—and continues to amuse and entertain more than thirty years later.

CRITICS' CIRCLE

"Despite the surface borrowings, *Charade* has an original quality of its own as it displays the sick elegance of a fashion show in a funeral parlor. With a plot that smells of red herrings, the picture is memorable for its irrelevant eccentricities—Audrey Hepburn, exquisitely emaciated in her Givenchy wardrobe; Cary Grant, more elfin than dolphin, taking a shower in his drip-dry suit; Walter Matthau doing setting-up exercises with the camera when he is not burping realistically as counterpoint to the ethereal Hepburn-Grant charade on sex. The saddest news of the year

CHARADE   With Walter Matthau

CHARADE   With Cary Grant

CHARADE   With Cary Grant

163

With Walter Matthau in *Charade*

is that Cary Dorian Grant is finally beginning to look his age."

—Andrew Sarris, *Village Voice*

"A handsomely wrapped package of fun and games, mayhem and murder, a twisting, twirling plot and a super-chilling chase climax and—glittering on top of it all—Audrey Hepburn and Cary Grant. The stars offer us a grown-up tongue-in-cheek romance. Peter Stone's script, abetted by Stanley Donen's direction, provides a whodunit that challenges both intellect and blood pressure, but is leavened by gentle and civilized comedy. Miss Hepburn has emerged from her Tom Sawyer–gamine stage as a breathtakingly beautiful woman. Good, gray Cary Grant is as debonair as ever and more than actor enough to make his potential villainies plausible despite his star status. He and Miss Hepburn make so charming a team that when the comedy lines fall flat, as they occasionally do, they seem to hear the thud first and shrug it off—as we do. Walter Matthau paints a neat portrait of a schemer, Jacques Marin is delightful, and George Kennedy, Ned Glass and James Coburn are a perfect trio of stupid hoods."

—Judith Crist, *New York Herald Tribune*

"The plot of *Charade* is exactly that, an enigma, in which a word of two or more syllables has to be guessed by a description of representation of the separate syllables and of the whole. In this case Grant is

With Cary Grant in *Charade*

CHARADE   Reggie runs for her life through the streets of Paris

the enigma, and the rest of the cast have to spend the entire film guessing at his function and purpose, for Grant is continually changing his identity to suit the circumstances. Too much cold logic turned on this story riddles it with implausibilities, but as the basis for sophisticated comedy it is eminently serviceable. Peter Stone's screenplay is full of excellent inventions, and his dialogue is barbed with a distinctive wit and style.

"Apart from the two stars, the actors only have to register baffled menace, which they all do excellently, but Grant and Hepburn foil each other sympathetically. Both employ the stiletto rather than the harpoon as the basis of their comic technique, and their ease and assurance together remind one of the vintage years of Hollywood comedy. Hepburn, an elegant ap-

CHARADE   With Cary Grant

CHARADE   Reggie finds temporary refuge in a prompter's box

parition in her Givenchy gowns, gives her usual distinctive performance, but Grant, skillfully handling some of the best material he's worked on in a long time, comes up with one of his happiest high-comedy performances (although even his impeccable comic technique can't carry him through an embarrassingly unfunny bit of mime in a shower). Slick, fast and funny, *Charade* is infinitely superior to Universal's other cash crop of comedies. It may not equal *The Trouble with Harry*, but it makes the Ross Hunter confections look like very stale pastries."

—Richard Whitehall, *Films and Filming*

"There's a lot to be said for it as a fast-moving, urbane entertainment in the comedy-mystery vein. Peter Stone has written a screenplay that is packed with sudden twists, shocking gags, eccentric arrangements and occasionally bright and brittle lines. And Stanley Donen has diligently directed in a style that is somewhere between that of the screwball comedy of the 1930s and that of Alfred Hitchcock on a *North by Northwest* course. The players have at it in a glib, polished, nonchalant way that clearly betrays their awareness of the film's howling implausibility. Miss Hepburn is cheerfully committed to a mood of hownuts-can-you-be in an obviously comforting assortment of Givenchy costumes, and Mr. Grant does everything with the blandness and boredom of an old screwball comedy hand. An interesting element in the picture is Henry Mancini's off-beat score, which makes the music a sardonic commentator."

—Bosley Crowther, *New York Times*

CHARADE   With
Cary Grant

166

Paris—When It Sizzles

CAST

William Holden (*Richard Benson*); Audrey Hepburn (*Gabrielle Simpson*); Grégoire Aslan (*Inspector Gillet*); Noël Coward (*Alexander Meyerheim*); Raymond Bussières (*Gangster*); Christian Duvalleix (*Maitre d'Hotel*); Tony Curtis (*Maurice/Philippe*); Thomas Michel (*Francois, the Chauffeur*); Marlene Dietrich (*Herself*); Dominique Boschero and Evi Marandi (*Girls at Meyerheim's Pool*); Mel Ferrer ("*Dr. Jekyll/Mr. Hyde*" Bit at Party).

CREDITS

Director: Richard Quine; *Producers*: Richard Quine and George Axelrod; *Associate Producers*: Carter De Haven and John R. Coonan; *Screenwriter*: George Axelrod; *Based on a story by* Julien Duvivier and Henri Jeanson, and the French film *La Fête à Henriette* (1951); *Panavision-Technicolor Cinematographers*: Charles Lang Jr. and (uncredited) Claude Renoir; *Special Photographic Effects*: Paul K. Lerpae; *Editor*: Archie Marshek; *Art Director*: Jean d'Eaubonne; *Set Decorator*: Gabriel Bechir; *Music*: Nelson Riddle; *Miss Hepburn's Wardrobe and Perfume*: Hubert de Givenchy; *Wardrobe Coordinator*: Jean Zay; *Running time*: 110 minutes. Available on videocassette.

ORIGINAL RELEASE

1964; a Paramount release of a Charleston Enterprises/Richard Quine production.

THE FILM

Audrey Hepburn's career hit a low point with this slight comedy that reunited her with *Sabrina*'s Wil-

PARIS WHEN IT SIZZLES With William Holden

168

liam Holden in a vehicle whipped up to fulfill contractual obligations between them and Paramount. And, in theory, there must have seemed wisdom in having *Breakfast at Tiffany*'s screenwriter George Axelrod make an Anglicized adaptation of a minor but well-received 1953 French comedy called *La Fête à Henriette* (*Holiday for Henrietta* in the U.S.), which would make Technicolored use of Parisian locations under the direction of Richard Quine, who had done so well by bringing *Bell, Book and Candle* from stage to screen a few years earlier. Axelrod and Quine also produced, and the results couldn't have been more disappointing, to put it gracefully. Its slim storyline puts Paris-based American screenwriter Holden in the position of having to put aside dissipated habits and pursue a commitment to movie producer Noël Coward by delivering the overdue script of something called *The Girl Who Stole the Eiffel Tower* within the next two days. To do so, Holden engages secretary Hepburn to assist in script preparations, with the result that they frantically set about inventing an

PARIS WHEN IT SIZZLES   With William Holden

appropriate screenplay, mostly by acting it out in a series of fantasy sequences.

Viewing the film some three decades later, one can only wince at its reflections of reality as Holden staggers about drunk while Hepburn tearfully chides him. In fact, the substantial presence of Tony Curtis in an uncredited, hastily concocted supporting role reportedly owes much to the filmmakers' need for "fill" during a week when Holden was "drying out" in a Paris clinic. But there is little that could save *Paris When It Sizzles*, and certainly not Audrey Hepburn's chic Givenchy wardrobe (on-screen credit attributes her *perfume* to her favorite French designer, as well). Filmed in 1962, the movie was temporarily shelved and released in 1964, after the subsequently shot *Charade*.

CRITICS' CIRCLE

"As accredited ribbers, George Axelrod and Richard Quine attempt to spoof the clichés of film writing and moviemaking, and only succeed in creating a Technicolored cliché themselves. . . . Miss Hepburn, sylphlike as ever in pastel-colored Givenchy frocks and tailleurs, is a willing heroine, but she seems slightly bewildered by the trumped-up zaniness in which she is involved. Mr. Holden, who is just as willing and properly frenzied as the anxious scenarist,

169

With William Holden in *Paris When It Sizzles* (1964)

PARIS WHEN IT SIZZLES   Gabrielle gets tipsy

the old French comedy *La Fête à Henriette*, on which it is based. In spite of its conscientiously 'Pareesian' backgrounds, it is essentially American in spirit, and the film take-offs, although they laboriously explore every cliché in the book, never really hit the target. But the heaviness of the film stems also from lack of joie de vivre in the playing. Neither of the principals seems to enjoy the joke much, and Audrey Hepburn especially strains too hard. She is not helped by the unsuitably adolescent wardrobe designed for her by Givenchy. There are bright moments from Tony Curtis

PARIS WHEN IT SIZZLES   Gabrielle gets a shock

shows signs of strain and a decided lack of conviction long before this pseudo-merry chase ends. In their breathless efforts at making *Paris* fashionable, smart and 'in,' Mr. Axelrod and Mr. Quine and their stars are not really inventive or funny. Even though they work up a great head of steam, *Paris When It Sizzles* is not so hot."

—A. H. Weiler, *New York Times*

"The latest of the current wave of would-be satirical 'film within a film' jokes has a slightly sour flavor which does not appear to have been inherited from

170

and Noël Coward, who put in guest appearances, and the dialogue is pleasantly literate, though less witty than one might expect from George Axelrod. Nevertheless, the overall impression is one of weariness and depression."

—"B. D.," *Monthly Film Bulletin*

"None of it, under Richard Quine's direction, has the slightest charm or humor. It's hard to determine which is worse: Axelrod's script or the various scripts he has Holden invent. Fatuous is perhaps the word that best describes the quality of the writing. One would hardly expect, then, that Miss Hepburn or Mr. Holden would be able to surmount the handicap of their basic material, and they do not. Their pretense of a light, kidding style is simply bad acting and, I guess, bad direction. The color photography makes Paris look lurid, and the whole venture amounts to a dreadfully expensive display of bad taste by the producers, Mr. Axelrod and Mr. Quine, who shouldn't have tried to improve on Duvivier."

—Hollis Alpert, *Saturday Review*

"They're handing us Audrey Hepburn and William Holden and Noël Coward and 'surprise' guest stars and Paris in every kind of color that goes with Bastille Day—and oh yes, 'Miss Hepburn's wardrobe and perfume by Hubert de Givenchy.' The wardrobe's so-so—but what we're smelling for nigh on to two hours isn't any Givenchy perfume.

"Now not, mind you, that there isn't potential in a satire on movie-writing. But the attempts at sophistication become ludicrous and the tedium unbearable as Holden and Hepburn enact endless parodies of Westerns, horror films, chase sequences, love scenes, extravaganzas—all of which we've seen done in far sharper, wittier and brighter form, let alone one-liners, by far brighter comedians.

"Miss Hepburn is, as always, very lovely to look at, and so is Paris. Mr. Holden, however, is not Cary Grant, even though he tries and he tries and he tries. And *Paris When It Sizzles*? Strictly Hollywood—when it fizzles."

—Judith Crist, *New York Herald Tribune*

"Contributions are in order from admirers of Audrey Hepburn to buy and suppress all copies of *Paris When It Sizzles*. It is based on an old Duvivier opus, which itself was deadly; the new script by George Axelrod embalms the original instead of reviving it. His dialogue and Holden's gift for comedy amply deserve each other. And in the midst of this meager harvest is Miss Audrey Hepburn trying to make chaff out of corn."

—Stanley Kauffmann, *New Republic*

PARIS WHEN IT SIZZLES With William Holden

171

My Fair Lady

MY FAIR LADY   With Rex Harrison

CAST

Audrey Hepburn (*Eliza Doolittle*, sung by Marni Nixon); Rex Harrison (*Prof. Henry Higgins*); Stanley Holloway (*Alfred Doolittle*); Wilfrid Hyde-White (*Col. Hugh Pickering*); Gladys Cooper (*Mrs. Higgins*); Jeremy Brett (*Freddie Eynsford-Hill*, sung by Bill Shirley); Theodore Bikel (*Zoltan Karpathy*); Mona Washbourne (*Mrs. Pearce*); Isobel Elsom (*Mrs. Eynsford-Hill*); John Holland (*Butler*); John Alderson (*Jamie*); John McLiam (*Harry*); Eric Heath and James O'Hara (*Costermongers*); Kendrick Huxham and Frank Baker (*Elegant Bystanders*); Walter Burke (*Main Bystander*); Queenie Leonard (*Cockney Bystander*); Laurie Main (*Hoxton Man*); Maurice Dallimore (*Selsey Man*); Owen McGiveney (*Man at Coffee Stand*); Marjorie Bennett (*Cockney with Pipe*); Jacqueline Squire (*Parlor Maid*); Gwen Watts (*Cook*); Roy Dean (*Footman*); Charles Fredericks (*King*); Lily Kemble-Cooper (*Lady Ambassador*); Barbara Pepper (*Doolittle's Dance Partner*); Aylene Gibbons (*Fat Woman at Pub*); Oscar Beregi (*Greek Ambassador*); Buddy Bryan (*Prince*); Moyna MacGill (*Lady Boxington*); Grady Sutton, Orville Sherman, Harvey Dunn, Barbara Morrison, Natalie Core, Helen Albrecht, and Diana Bourbon (*Ascot Types*); Alan Napier (*Ambassador*); Geoffrey Steele (*Taxi Driver*); Henry Daniell (*Prince Gregor of Transylvania*).

CREDITS

Director: George Cukor; *Producer*: Jack L. Warner; *Screenwriter*: Alan Jay Lerner; *Based on the musical play by* Alan Jay Lerner (*Book and Lyrics*) and Frederick Loewe (*Music*) *and the play* Pygmalion *by* George Bernard Shaw; *Technicolor-Super Panavision 70 Cinematographer*: Harry Stradling; *Editor*: William Ziegler; *Production and Costume Designer*: Cecil Beaton; *Art Director*: Gene Allen; *Set Decorator*: George

As Eliza Doolittle in *My Fair Lady* (1964)

James Hopkins; *Choreographer*: Hermes Pan; *Songs*:
"Why Can't the English?" "Wouldn't It Be Loverly?"
"I'm an Ordinary Man," "With a Little Bit of Luck,"
"Just You Wait," "The Servant's Chorus," "The Rain
in Spain," "I Could Have Danced All Night," "Ascot
Gavotte," "On the Street Where You Live," "The
Embassy Waltz," "You Did It," "Show Me," "The
Flower Market," "Get Me to the Church on Time,"
"A Hymn to Him," "Without You," and "I've Grown
Accustomed to Her Face". *Running time*: 170 min-
utes. Available on videocassette and laser disc.

ORIGINAL RELEASE

1964; a Warner Brothers Picture.

THE FILM

George Bernard Shaw's play *Pygmalion* is probably
best known today for its memorable 1938 British
screen version with Leslie Howard as the crusty, bachelor speech professor Henry Higgins, and Wendy
Hiller as Eliza Doolittle, the Cockney flower-seller
who challenges her mentor's makeover powers, before
eventually passing for a lady in London society. The
film's producer, Gabriel Pascal, later unsuccessfully
tried to persuade Shaw that his work had the makings
of a delightful musical comedy, and it wasn't until

after the playwright's death in 1950 that Pascal was
able to enlist the interest of either West End or Broad-
way tunesmiths. Amazingly, the concept was turned
down by no less than Noël Coward, Cole Porter, and
E. Y. Harburg, before Richard Rodgers and Oscar
Hammerstein II gave it a try—and admitted defeat.
More successful, however, was the team of Alan Jay
Lerner and Frederick Loewe, who already had *Briga-
doon* and *Paint Your Wagon* to their credit. As a
work-in-progress, it bore the interim title *My Fair
Liza*, and was at one time being tailored for Mary
Martin—until she rejected the project because she
didn't like its score! As *My Fair Lady*, the musical
arrived on Broadway in the spring of 1956, picking
up a bundle of Tony Awards, as well as the New York
Drama Critics Circle Award as Best Musical of 1956.
It ran for an impressive 2,717 performances.

Warner Brothers' Jack L. Warner was sufficiently
aware of the show's screen potential to sanction a
record expenditure of $5.5 million for the rights, and
another $12 million to produce the movie. And al-
though Rex Harrison had won a Tony for his talk-
singing portrayal of Higgins, Warner initially tried to
sign Cary Grant for the film. Grant's rejoinder was
that, if Harrison didn't get to repeat his stage creation,
he (Grant) would not even *attend* the motion picture.
Nor would second-choice Rock Hudson consider the

role. And so Harrison was engaged, although he was then considered passé as a box-office attraction. But there was absolutely no interest at Warners in hiring Broadway's delightful Julie Andrews, who had never made a movie, to re-create her stage Eliza for Hollywood, although executive producer Jack Warner could have secured her services for a bargain $75,000. Instead, they selected Audrey Hepburn, a box-office favorite, who cost the studio all of a million dollars, as well as the necessity of a vocal double. Hepburn recorded some of Eliza's songs but, by her own admission, was "no soprano." Thus, a high-flying number like "I Could Have Danced All Night" was assuredly beyond her capabilities. And Marni Nixon, who had already done an admirable job of "singing for" Natalie Wood in *West Side Story* and Deborah Kerr in *The King and I*, sang again for Hepburn. Audrey's own throaty voice, revealed in a 1994 behind-the-scenes documentary about *My Fair Lady*'s restoration, is quite charming, albeit on a less professional level.

Hepburn's casting, of course, helped guarantee a movie audience for this expensive enterprise, despite some negative industry feelings that a nonsinger had been cast to replace an acclaimed New York star whose name meant little in Los Angeles. As for Julie Andrews, Walt Disney signed her for $125,000 to star in *Mary Poppins*, for which she eventually won

MY FAIR LADY   With Rex Harrison

1964's Best Actress Academy Award—an honor for which Audrey Hepburn wasn't even *nominated* for *My Fair Lady*.

My Fair Lady cost Warners a then-lofty $17 million to produce, but it made a profit of $12 million, a sum now commanded by some of nineties Hollywood's biggest male stars—for a single picture!

My Fair Lady garnered no less than twelve Oscar nominations, and proved that year's champion, winning eight statuettes, including Best Picture, Best Actor (Harrison), and Best Director (George Cukor), as well as for cinematography, art direction/set decoration, sound, scoring, and costume design. Cecil Beaton's contract guaranteed his receiving credit for the

Dancing to "The Rain in Spain" with Rex Harrison from *My Fair Lady*

design of both "production" and costumes, although it was later revealed that only the film's striking wardrobe was attributable to Beaton. *My Fair Lady*'s equally impressive sets were by the man officially credited for its "art direction," Gene Allen.

Cast in the film as Freddy Eynsford-Hill, the male ingenue of sorts who sings "On the Street Where You Live," was Jeremy Brett. Contemporary TV audiences now know him as Sherlock Holmes on the long-running PBS Conan Doyle series.

In a 1991 interview, Audrey Hepburn talked about her once controversial *My Fair Lady* casting: "I understood the dismay of people who had seen Julie on Broadway. Julie made that role her own, and for that

MY FAIR LADY   With Stanley Holloway and Rex Harrison

reason I didn't want to do the film when it was first offered. But Jack Warner never wanted to put Julie in the film. He was totally opposed to it, for whatever reason. Then I learned that if I turned it down, they would offer it to still another movie actress. So I felt I should have the same opportunity to play it as any other film actress."

And if some audiences were disappointed with Hepburn's performance, many others were not. Following her death in 1993, not a few of the many memorial press tributes ran variations on *Entertainment Weekly*'s headline—"Farewell, Fair Lady."

CRITICS' CIRCLE

"As Henry Higgins might have whooped, 'By George, they've got it!' They've made a superlative film from the musical stage show *My Fair Lady*—a film that enchantingly conveys the rich endowments of the famous stage production in a fresh and flowing cinematic form. . . . All things considered, it is the brilliance of Miss Hepburn as the Cockney waif who is transformed by Prof. Henry Higgins into an elegant female facade that gives an extra touch of subtle

MY FAIR LADY   Audrey poses for Cecil Beaton's camera in a non-Eliza Beaton creation

magic and individuality to the film. What Miss Hepburn brings is a fine sensitivity of feeling and a phenomenal histrionic skill. Her Covent Garden flower girl is not just a doxy of the streets. She's a terrifying example of the elemental self-assertion of the female sex.

"Miss Hepburn is most expressive in the beautiful scenes where she achieves the manners and speech of a lady, yet fails to achieve that one thing she needs for a sense of belonging—that is, the recognition of the man she loves. She is dazzlingly beautiful and comic in the crisply satiric Ascot scene played almost precisely as it was on the stage. She is stiffly serene and distant at the embassy ball and almost unbearably poignant in the later scenes when she hungers for love. Mr. Cukor has maneuvered Miss Hepburn and Mr. Harrison so deftly in these scenes that he has one perpetually alternating between chuckling laughter and dabbing the moisture from one's eyes. Though it runs for three hours—or close to it—this *My Fair Lady* seems to fly past like a breeze."

—Bosley Crowther, *New York Times*

MY FAIR LADY   With Gladys Cooper, Jeremy Brett, Rex Harrison, and Wilfrid Hyde-White

MY FAIR LADY   Eliza on her own

"Rex Harrison, who played Henry Higgins for two years on Broadway and one year in London, repeats his original role, and thank heavens for that; no one, but no one, could possibly have been just as right as he is in the part of the charmingly, elegantly arrogant phonetics professor who transforms a bedraggled little flower girl into a grand lady. Harrison's performance is a delight in both the straight scenes and in the musical numbers, and he does full justice to Lerner's witty lyrics in those memorable songs, from 'I'm an Ordinary Man' to 'I've Grown Accustomed to Her Face.'

"Audrey Hepburn is an enchanting Eliza Doolittle, and if her interpretation of the role is different from that of Julie Andrews, that was only to be expected. She's amusing as the Cockney ragamuffin and radiantly lovely when she climbs from grime to glamor;

MY FAIR LADY   Eliza at the embassy ball

whether or not she does her own singing, she put over her song numbers most engagingly, especially when learning to say properly 'The Rain in Spain' or whirling about to the strains of 'I Could Have Danced All Night.'

"George Cukor has done a marvelous job of bringing together all the elements that made *My Fair Lady* the most successful stage musical in Broadway history, and at the same time handling them with such cinematic skill that the film never becomes simply a photographed stage show."

—Rose Pelswick, *New York Journal-American*

"The Lerner and Loewe musical staggers along in this large production, directed by George Cukor and designed by Cecil Beaton. The film seems to go on for about forty-five minutes after the story is finished. Audrey Hepburn is an affecting Eliza, though she is totally unconvincing as a guttersnipe, and is made to sing with that dreadfully impersonal Marni Nixon voice that has issued from so many other screen stars. Rex Harrison had already played Higgins more than a bit too often."

—Pauline Kael, *5001 Nights at the Movies*

"Probably no man alive has seen all the Eliza Doolittles since George Bernard Shaw put her on the stage in his 1912 *Pygmalion*, which inspired the musical. Nevertheless, I am laying bets Audrey Hepburn must be the most delightful in the long procession of Elizas. Every movie Audrey makes seems exquisitely right. Her wit is delivered with sure instinct for wringing the last ounce of laughter. Her volcanic and hilarious wrath is always smoldering. Tiny [sic] Audrey is fragile as well as formidable, the endearing foil for a professorial prank that erupts into a ferociously cruel aftermath. Her pathos may be tearful but it comes across as happy sympathy down in the audience."

—Alton Cook, *New York World-Telegram*

MY FAIR LADY   With Rex Harrison

(*On facing page*) With Rex Harrison in *My Fair Lady*

MY FAIR LADY   The embassy ball

"In one sense, it must all have been very easy: with the range of talent, taste and sheer professionalism at work, from Shaw onwards, Warners could hardly have made a film which would do less than please most of the people most of the time. What almost does this trick is Rex Harrison's domineering, cantankerous Higgins, a performance definitive in its intelligence, bullying charm, and relish of every Shavian insult. Audrey Hepburn can't manage the guttersnipe, and is not the first Eliza to give the impression that it's the Cockney that has been learned from an elocutionist. But from the tea-table dialogue, done with deadpan precision so that every awful word strikes home, she takes a firm hold on the part. *Pygmalion*, really, is a confidence trick, in that Shaw left out the real business of transforming Eliza, from the tea-party to the ball. The actress has to make an impossible transition work, and Miss Hepburn's fragile triumph and disconsolate rage are very touching.

—"P. H.," *Monthly Film Bulletin*

"It is Hollywood at its best. Only incurably disputatious persons will consider it a defect of *Lady* on screen that Julie Andrews has been replaced by the better known Miss H. She is thoroughly beguiling as Eliza, though her singing is dubbed by Marni Nixon. There is hardly a dull moment and, more to the point, there are many laughs, many humanly touching scenes, and song numbers that come smashing through. This is an occasion for general congratulations. Hollywood has seldom looked lovelier."

—"Land.," *Variety*

MY FAIR LADY   With Rex Harrison

With John Holland, Wilfrid Hyde-White, and Rex Harrison

184

How to Steal a Million

As Nicole Bonnet in *How to Steal a Million*

CAST
Audrey Hepburn (*Nicole Bonnet*); Peter O'Toole (*Simon Dermott*); Eli Wallach (*David Leland*); Hugh Griffith (*Charles Bonnet*); Charles Boyer (*De Solnay*); Fernand Gravey (*Grammont*); Marcel Dalio (*Señor Paravideo*); Jacques Marin (*Chief Guard*); Moustache (*Guard*); Roger Treville (*Auctioneer*); Eddie Malin (*Insurance Clerk*); Bert Bertram (*Marcel*).

CREDITS
Director: William Wyler; *Producer*: Fred Kohlmar; *Second-Unit Director and Editor*: Robert Swink; *Screenwriter*: Harry Kurnitz; *Based on a Story by* George Bradshaw; *DeLuxe Color–Panavision Cinematographer*: Charles Lang; *Production Designer*: Alexander Trauner; *Music*: Johnny Williams; *Miss Hepburn's Wardrobe*: Hubert de Givenchy; *Running time*: 127 minutes. Available on videocassette.

ORIGINAL RELEASE
1966; a Twentieth Century–Fox release of a World Wide–William Wyler production.

THE FILM
How to Steal a Million started out as a project entitled *Venus Rising*, after the George Bradshaw short story from which it is derived, and was known through much of its production by the unwieldy tab of *How to Steal a Million Dollars and Live Happily Ever After*. Its derivative plotline owed something to many of Audrey Hepburn's earlier films, as well as to such sixties museum-heist caper movies as *Topkapi* and *Gambit*. And again, Paris was the locale of a Hepburn movie. This time, she's the daughter of a clever, third-generation art forger (Hugh Griffith), who makes the mistake of allowing his brilliantly bogus "Cellini Venus" to be displayed in a small Paris museum. When she learns that government officials are to appraise the statue, now on display and thus temporarily out of their hands, Hepburn blackmails a "society burglar" (Peter O'Toole) to help her steal the statue from the museum. And although he's really an art *detective* on the trail of her nefarious father, O'Toole is already so smitten with her that he goes along with the burglary plan. He then employs ingenious methods to replace the false Cellini from its laser-

HOW TO STEAL A MILLION   With Hugh Griffith

HOW TO STEAL A MILLION   With Peter O'Toole

alarm-protected pedestal, where he leaves a half-consumed wine bottle in its place. Meanwhile, the wealthy American art collector (Eli Wallach) who had earlier wanted to marry Hepburn shows his true character when he elects to give her up for a chance to purchase the false Cellini. And so Hepburn and O'Toole wind up altar-bound, and Griffith plots the creation of his next "Old Master."

The film began production with George C. Scott signed for the Wallach role, but director William Wyler fired Scott for failing to adhere to the Parisian shooting schedule. Commenting years later on the abrupt dismissal, Wyler said, "In any case, it was no reflection on his ability, and it surely had no effect on his career."

For this return to contemporary roles, following her Eliza Doolittle, Hepburn sported a very different look from her earlier sixties motion pictures: With her hair radically cut in the style of a helmetlike beehive, the actress's unforgettable face here takes on a somewhat harder appearance, an effect reinforced by exaggerated eyeliner that unduly distracts. Nor does the severity of her hairstyle soften Hepburn's profile, an aspect of her screen persona about which she was always particularly self-conscious. And once again, she was clothed in a becomingly chic wardrobe designed by Hubert de Givenchy—except for the scene where she masks as a drab museum charwoman. With everything thus set for an inside joke, there's a sly exchange between O'Toole and Hepburn that begins with his line "That does it." "Does what?" she inquires. To which he replies, "Well, it gives Givenchy the night off."

How to Steal a Million was Audrey Hepburn's third and last film under the direction of William Wyler, who would next cope with a more formidable project—Barbra Streisand's *Funny Girl.*

CRITICS' CIRCLE

"Wyler's work may have become increasingly impersonal during the past decade or so, yet nothing he has done of late is quite so anonymous as the present film. This would not have mattered so much if the material had been strong enough to stand on its own feet, but it needs a much finer sophistication and drive than Wyler has brought to it: in short it really required another director. The trouble lies in that mid-Sixties Hollywood malaise: a verbose and relatively unwitty script which takes an unconscionable time to get under way. Audrey Hepburn, very fetchingly gowned, gives her usual warm impersonation of wide-eyed, guileful innocence; Peter O'Toole, although trying less hard than usual, tends to be more winsome than winning; and Hugh Griffith does another of his bearded old rogues. All fail to bring much zip or charm to the dialogue exchanges, and only Eli Wallach as the zany American tycoon looks as if he is really enjoying overacting.

"The robbery sequence (apart from some obvious plot loopholes) is quite ingeniously sustained, even though we have seen those funny French policemen once too often before. Also, for a film made in Paris, it is remarkably short on genuine locations, and the print quality, with its thick colour and muddy dissolves, presumably does scant justice to Charles Lang's camerawork."

"J. G.," *Monthly Film Bulletin*

"Meticulous high comedy. The fawnlike look is Audrey's special domain as a comedienne, and her partner in crime on this elegant occasion is Peter O'Toole, also treading very lightly as a debonair art-world detective. *How to Steal a Million* is tastefully

HOW TO STEAL A MILLION As Nicole Bonnet

HOW TO STEAL A MILLION With Peter O'Toole

187

As Nicole Bonnet in *How to Steal a Million* (1966)

"*How to Steal a Million* returns William Wyler to the enchanting province of his *Roman Holiday*. Making a sharp change of pace from the director's product of recent years, this is an entertaining treat which should captivate every type audience.

—"Whit.," *Variety*

"An old master, William Wyler, indulges himself in some suspense in *How to Steal a Million*, but he plays it for wit and comedy, and is aided by the stylish work of Audrey Hepburn and Peter O'Toole, an engaging pair. Most of the fun revolves around their efforts in getting a phony Cellini sculpture out of a maximum-security Paris museum. Both do their best with the lines provided by Harry Kurnitz, whose wit too often is on the ethereal side, and Wyler's

directed and competently performed, but its glossy tone somehow brushes out any forward momentum. In a film that cries out for wild hilarity and a heady spirit of adventure, everything that is going to happen happens according to long-established rules of the game, from the first skittish encounter to the last eager kiss. Its old-fashioned fun looks over-practiced, becoming merely another workout for a troupe of talented professionals who do their jobs with coolly measured skill, rather than warm-blooded will."

—*Time*

"An expensive cast in an anemic suspense comedy-romance. William Wyler directed from a rather tired screenplay by Harry Kurnitz. The picture isn't offensive, and it's handsome enough, but it's just blah."

—Pauline Kael, *5001 Nights at the Movies*

"An absolute strawberry-shortcake of a film, with Audrey Hepburn and Peter O'Toole an utterly delightful pair of respectable thieves and with Eli Wallach and Hugh Griffith on hand to steal scenes. The whipped cream of Paris in color covers the attenuation of trivia."

—Judith Crist on NBC's *Today* show

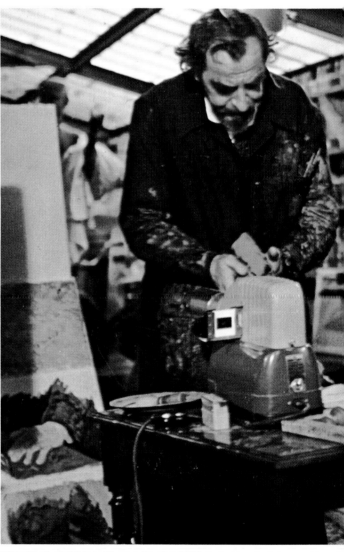

With Hugh Griffith in *How to Steal a Million*

direction is polished, if not very exciting. But to help maintain interest there's some expert comic performing by Hugh Griffith and Eli Wallach, and Givenchy has decked out Miss Hepburn in several truly eye-catching costumes."

—Hollis Alpert, *Saturday Review*

"How strangely derivative the whole thing is. At casual first glance it looks like another of those lovely figures for gamine and guy, played breezily in Paris or Rome: *Love in the Afternoon, Gigi, Sabrina, Roman Holiday*. Casting accounts for much of the sense of déjà vu. Audrey Hepburn is at it again, dressed to the nines by Givenchy, bejeweled by Cartier, terribly chic and terribly anxious to protect that irrepressible old forger of a father."

—*Newsweek*

"Absolute, unabashed deception, not only as a plot element but as a method of wooing the audience into charmed and uncontentious belief, is beautifully and cheerfully practiced in this wholly ingratiating film that should leave everyone who sees it feeling kindlier about deceit. Of course, you are not expected to believe it. The whole thing is clearly preposterous. Never mind. It is still a delightful lot of flummery while it is going on, especially the major, central business of burglarizing the museum. Remember that burglary in *Topkapi*? Well, this is a parody of it—only a parody so deft and delicious it might be an original. It consists of exquisite preparations, a wonderfully wry, romantic scene of Mr. O'Toole and Miss Hepburn discovering love in a broom-closet in the museum (in which they prove, incidentally, to be the most seductive whisperers in films); a grand lot of Keystone Cop clowning by Jacques Marin as the chief museum guard, and a comical performance of a flatfoot by Moustache. Cheers all around for everybody—for Miss Hepburn, Mr. O'Toole, Mr. Griffith, Mr. Wallach, and for the scriptwriter Harry Kurnitz, and especially for William Wyler, who directed with humor and style. So let me be serious in conclusion: art may not be deceit, but this is certainly an instance in which deception comes out a kind of art."

—Bosley Crowther, *New York Times*

With Peter O'Toole in *How to Steal a Million*

Two for the Road

TWO FOR THE ROAD   As Joanna Wallace

CAST

Audrey Hepburn (*Joanna Wallace*); Albert Finney (*Mark Wallace*); Eleanor Bron (*Cathy Manchester*); William Daniels (*Howard Manchester*); Claude Dauphin (*Maurice Dalbret*); Nadia Gray (*Francoise Dalbret*); Georges Descrieres (*David*); Gabrielle Middleton (*Ruth*); Kathy Chelimsky (*Caroline*); Carol Van Dyke (*Michelle*); Karyn Balm (*Simone*); Mario Verdon (*Palamos*); Roger Dann (*Gilbert*); Irene Hilda (*Yvonne de Florac*); Dominique Joos (*Sylvia*); Libby Morris (*American Lady*); Yves Barsacq (*Police Inspector*); Helene Tossy (*Hotel Proprietor*); Jean-Francois Lalet (*Boat Officer*); Albert Michel (*Customs Officer*); Jackie (Jacqueline) Bisset, Joanna Jones, Judy Cornwell, Sofia Torkeli, Patricia Viterbo, Olga George Picot, and Clarissa Hillel (*Joanna's Touring Girlfriends*).

CREDITS

Producer-Director: Stanley Donen; *Associate Producer*: Jimmy Ware; *Production Executive*: Arthur Carroll; *Production Supervisor*: Christian Ferry; *Screenwriter*: Frederic Raphael; *DeLuxe Color–Panavision Cinematographer*: Christopher Challis; *Editors*: Richard Marden and Madeleine Gug; *Art Directors*: Willy Holt and Marc Frederix; *Set Decorator*: Roger Volper; *Special Effects*: Gilbert Manzon; *Aerial Cameraman*: Guy Tabary; *Wardrobe Coordinator*: Sophie Issartel Rochas; *Miss Hepburn's Wardrobe*: Ken Scott, Michele Rosier, Paco Rabanne, Mary Quant, and Foale and Tuffin; *Mr. Finney's Wardrobe*: Hardy Amies; *Music*: Henry Mancini; *Running time*: 112 minutes. Available on videocassette and laser disc.

ORIGINAL RELEASE

1967; a Twentieth Century–Fox release of a Stanley Donen production.

THE FILM

This offbeat "road" picture marked the third and final collaboration between Audrey Hepburn and producer-director Stanley Donen—always among her most congenial working relationships. The unusual script was an original by Britain's Oscar-winning Frederic Raphael (*Darling*), focusing on the rocky marital relationship of an English couple over the course of twelve years, as they take motor-trip vacations through the south of France. The movie's most unusual aspect is its nonlinear construction, with regard to time sequence, for the couple is shown in alternating periods of their relationship, jumping back and forth over the years. Keeping audience confusion to a minimum, Donen is careful to establish his separate time periods via an astute attention to hairstyles, costuming, and automobiles, as architect Mark Wallace and his wife Joanna become increasingly more affluent and have a child. If Hepburn comes off better than Finney, undoubtedly it's because her role is better written. But it's also possible that she may have been the better actor; certainly, Finney's flat, monotonous vocal patterns hardly encourage audience interest or sympathy. It seems difficult to believe that, at thirty-eight, Audrey Hepburn was seven years Finney's senior, for they look very good together, perhaps the result of such offscreen rapport that rumors of an affair prevailed in the gossip columns during *Two for the Road*'s production. One can only speculate how different the movie might have been had Donen's original choice for Mark—Michael Caine—been available at the time. Years later, Caine remarked that it was the one role he regretted losing out on.

Since her favorite designer, Givenchy, would not have been an appropriate choice for *Two for the Road*, Hepburn substituted the boutique designs of continental names like Mary Quant and Paco Rabanne, and she's particularly fetching in a trendy party dress made out of metallic discs. But it's also a welcome change to see her in less formal attire, from jeans and bathing suits to leather pants. And, if she repeats her beehive helmet hairstyle from *How to Steal a Million*, the actress also runs the gamut of simpler, more becoming hairdos.

Over the years, *Two for the Road*, with its especially lovely Mancini title tune, has become something of a cult favorite, with a very devoted following for a film that offers its audiences a great deal if they are

TWO FOR THE ROAD   With Albert Finney

TWO FOR THE ROAD   With Albert Finney

191

TWO FOR THE ROAD   With Albert Finney

TWO FOR THE ROAD   With Albert Finney and Georges Descrieres

willing to pay close attention, for it's not a movie to wander in and out of. Perhaps, in a way, it was too special for 1967, for *Two for the Road* won no prizes. In fact, its only Academy Award nomination was for Frederic Raphael's original screenplay—and that Oscar went to William Rose for *Guess Who's Coming to Dinner*. Audrey Hepburn *was* nominated, but for *Wait Until Dark*, released later that same year. Belatedly saluting her portrayal of Joanna Wallace from the perspective of the mid-seventies, producer Richard Zanuck named it the best by an American actress during the sixties.

CRITICS' CIRCLE

"*Two for the Road* is that rare thing, an adult comedy by and for grown-ups, bright, brittle and sophisticated, underlined by cogency and honest emotion. And, far from coincidentally, it is a complex and beautifully made movie, eye-filling and engrossing with a 'new' (mod and non-Givenchy) Audrey Hepburn displaying her too-long-neglected depths and scope as an actress, and Albert Finney, after too long an absence from the screen, making us appreciate once again and with a fresh eye the talents of this fine young actor. Written by Frederic Raphael, whose *Nothing But the Best* and *Darling* scenarios demonstrated his way with a wit and his eye for the workings of today's society, *Two for the Road* is, in concept, a sort of four-wheeler version of *The Fourposter*. In execution, it is a complex interweaving of flashbacks, a varied and subtle and lighthearted exploration of how love leads to marriage, and how love and marriage change over the years.

—Judith Crist, *New York World Journal Tribune*

"Abandoning the Givenchy school and the elfin cool, Audrey Hepburn is surprisingly good as a Virginia Woolf-cub who has earned her share of scars in the jungle war between the sexes. As her mate, Albert Finney is not so fortunate, and seems curiously unsympathetic in helping to turn his marriage into a fray-for-all. Happily, whenever the strife skitters closer to tragedy than comedy, Director Stanley Donen takes the viewer's eye off the brawl by ushering in William Daniels and Eleanor Bron parodying a WASPish American and his shrewish wife, or Claude Dauphin, whose jet-set bore is a perfect put-down. Frederic Raphael, who won a 1965 Academy Award for *Darling*, has written a script that makes up in salt what it lacks in plot. Flashing back and forth through twelve years of togetherness and apartheid, Director Donen makes sure that this articulate *Road* never quite reaches a dead end. In the final moments, Hepburn and Finney, reconciled, look lovingly at each other in the car. He sighs, 'Bitch." She snaps, 'Bastard.' In its own perverse way, it's a happy ending, and one with a moral: a husband and a wife always have a chance to make a go of it as long as they can laugh at a single private joke—even if the joke is marriage."

—*Time*

"Miss Hepburn moves swiftly but gently through all the manifestations of virginity to marriage and womanhood, hardly missing any of the in-between stages. She is delicate and responsive in her performance, alternately seductive and aggressive, playing the theme of the joys and agonies of love to her womanly hilt."

Independent Film Journal

"*Two for the Road* is perhaps the best American movie of 1967, even with its occasional lapses into Hollywood formula lushness. But overlooking its oversized budget and some of Director Stanley Donen's self-conscious camera trickeries, you will be rewarded with a moving, disturbing, strikingly adult comment on modern marriage, written by Frederic Raphael, and by two of the most brilliant performances—by

As Joanna Wallace in *Two for the Road* (1967)

With Albert Finney in
Two for the Road

193

Audrey Hepburn and Albert Finney—ever captured on the screen. Hepburn and Finney are such a dream combination that they visually achieve such revelations of character, atmosphere, and emotion that their freshness and originality give the film a kind of vitality and continuance that seems easy. It is only much later that their brilliance begins to overtake you. They are aided, of course, by Raphael's script—funny, warm, juicy, rich—with serious undertones of now people and now relationships."

—Rex Reed, *Big Screen, Little Screen*

"Despite its high-toned trimmings, a film like this must stand or fall by its stars, and the leading players are here well worth watching, even if they are never quite able to get beneath the skins of the characters they portray. Albert Finney, apart from some uneasy attempts to impersonate Humphrey Bogart, almost manages to bring off the frequent sharp transitions from youthful student to young married to discontented successful architect and back again. Audrey Hepburn, in a dashing wardrobe by Ken Scott, Michele Rosier, Paco Rabanne, Mary Quant, Foale and Tiffin, 'and others' (it is, after all, really that kind of film), successfully rings the changes from youthful

candour to bored bitchiness and finally more mature understanding.

"Stanley Donen here once more proves himself an adroit craftsman and a supreme entertainer."

—"J. I.," *Monthly Film Bulletin*

"All this is diverting enough, if not sensationally enjoyable, and I suppose it's the calculation behind it that keeps the adventure from sparking into vivid life. Miss Hepburn is handicapped during her more immature periods by the fact that she is now a distinctly aging ingenue, and someone of her delicate bone structure just shouldn't wear such brief swimsuits. And Finney seems too young to play a mature architect. But fashion, in stars as well as clothes and cars, must be served by Donen, and the trouble with *Two for the Road* is that it is."

—Hollis Alpert, *Saturday Review*

"A breezy trip through married life with Audrey Hepburn's superb performance carrying stodgy Albert Finney most of the way. What must have been a tremendous challenge to producer-director Stanley Donen is the script dreamed up by Frederic Raphael, which has the same married couple, making basically

TWO FOR THE ROAD   With Albert Finney

the same trip, from London to the Riviera, at three different stages of their life with continual cross-cutting and flashing backwards and forwards from one period to the other. The credibility of the changes in periods is left, except for the changes in costume and vehicular equipment, to the two leads. Finney remains the same throughout, but Miss Hepburn is amazing in her ability to portray a very young girl, a just-pregnant wife of two years, and a beginning-to-be-bored wife of five years. Helped partially by variations in her hairdos but mostly by her facial expressions, she's completely believable, lovable and totally delightful. A major asset is the score by Henry Mancini, one of the most romantic he's done to date. A refreshing change is that there's no title tune sung during the credits."

—"Robe.," *Variety*

TWO FOR THE ROAD   With Albert Finney

195

WAIT UNTIL DARK   With Efrem Zimbalist Jr.

WAIT UNTIL DARK   With a disguised Alan Arkin

WAIT UNTIL DARK   With Richard Crenna

Wait Until Dark

CAST

Audrey Hepburn (*Susy Hendrix*); Alan Arkin (*Roat*); Richard Crenna (*Mike Talman*); Efrem Zimbalist Jr. (*Sam Hendrix*); Jack Weston (*Carlino*); Julie Herrod (*Gloria*); Frank O'Brien (*Shatner*); Samantha Jones (*Lisa*); Gary Morgan (*The Boy*).

CREDITS

Director: Terence Young; *Executive Producer*: Walter MacEwen; *Producer*: Mel Ferrer; *Screenwriters*: Robert and Jane-Howard Carrington; *Based on the play by Frederick Knott; Technicolor Cinematographer*: Charles Lang; *Editor*: Gene Milford; *Art Director*: George Jenkins; *Set Decorator*: George James Hopkins; *Music*: Henry Mancini; *Title-Song Lyrics*: Jay Livingston and Ray Evans; *Sung by* Bobby Darin; *Running time*: 108 minutes. Available on videocassette and laser disc.

ORIGINAL RELEASE

1967; a Warner Brothers–Seven Arts Picture.

THE FILM

Frederick Knott's Broadway thriller opened in February 1966 and ran for a profitable 372 performances

As Susy Hendrix in *Wait Until Dark* (1967)

before becoming a popular staple on the summer-theater circuit. When its 1967 screen version was planned, none of the stage cast (Lee Remick, Robert Duvall, Mitchell Ryan, James Congdon, and Val Bisoglio) was retained, except for young Julie Herrod, as Gloria, the little girl who lives upstairs. But where the play remained confined to the Greenwich Village apartment of photographer Sam Hendrix and his blind wife, Susy, the movie began in Montreal, where the audience views the setup for a crime: A glamorous blonde named Lisa (Samantha Jones) prepares to head for the airport, where she smuggles a stash of heroin through customs hidden inside a child's doll. But her behavior turns furtive when her plane lands in New York and she recognizes someone waiting for her; acting quickly, she prevails upon fellow passenger Sam Hendrix (Efrem Zimbalist Jr.) to keep the doll for her temporarily. Then she walks off with the individual who initially gave her pause—a sinister-looking man with dark glasses. Thus, screenwriters Robert and Jane-Howard Carrington set the scene for suspense and an intriguing chain of events that will center on a basement apartment on St. Luke's Place in the Village, where its chief players will be Sam's trusting wife, Susy (Audrey Hepburn), and a ruthless man of many voices named Roat (Alan Arkin). Suffice it to report that the now-missing heroin provides the motive, and that the plot's clever twists should not be further detailed here.

With Mel Ferrer this time producing and Britain's veteran Terence Young directing, *Wait Until Dark* provided an ideal vehicle for Audrey Hepburn, who visited New York City's Lighthouse for the Blind School to prepare for her role. But because her eyes were deemed too expressive in their natural state, Young had her fitted with uncomfortable contact lenses, which she was forced to endure throughout the film's production, part of which was shot in its fictional Manhattan setting. When she was forbidden to commission a Givenchy wardrobe, Hepburn selected the film's comfort-oriented sports clothing from the racks amid a shopping excursion to Paris. Thus, the film bears no costume-design credits.

Surprisingly (to some), the actress's rapport with her fellow cast members exceeded that between star Hepburn and producer Ferrer, for their marriage was then going through its painful final stage, with divorce to follow soon thereafter. It would be her last movie for almost a decade. *Wait Until Dark* scored big at the box office and earned Audrey Hepburn her fifth and final Academy Award nomination among competition that included Anne Bancroft in *The Graduate*, Faye Dunaway in *Bonnie and Clyde*, Dame Edith Evans in *The Whisperers*—and that year's winner, *Katharine* Hepburn, for *Guess Who's Coming to Dinner*

CRITICS' CIRCLE

"Examined closely, the story is as full of holes as a kitchen colander. Though the housewife has been sightless less than a year, she has already developed incredibly acute hearing and a sixth sense of unseen danger. Still, Audrey Hepburn's honest, posture-free performance helps to suspend the audience's disbelief. She is immensely aided by the heavies: Jack Weston, Richard Crenna, and Alan Arkin playing his first straight roles—triple portrayals of a Peter Lorre–like psychopathic killer, a white-haired father and his smarmy son."

—*Time*

"Patience is strongly recommended for those who see *Wait Until Dark*—patience with the slow and tortuous build-up to the chilling denouement and patience with some of the doubtful details of the clearly carpentered plot. But once this build-up is accomplished, the shock and suspense of the situation hit the audience. And from here on, the tension is terrific and the melodramatic action is wild as the blind woman uses all her courage and ingenuity to foil her assailants and save her life.

"It is just that, a barefaced malodrama, without character revelation of any sort, outside the demonstration of a person with the fortitude to overcome an infirmity. But the sweetness with which Miss Hepburn plays the poignant role, the quickness with which she changes and the skill with which she manifests terror attract sympathy and anxiety to her and give her genuine solidity in the final scenes. But I must say that I found Mr. Arkin a bit disconcerting at times, when he seemed like his comical self imitating Jerry Lewis imitating a tough-talking thug."

—Bosley Crowther, *New York Times*

"*Wait Until Dark* emerges as an excellent suspense drama, effective in casting, scripting, direction and genuine emotional impact. Audrey Hepburn stars in

WAIT UNTIL DARK   With Richard Crenna, Jack Weston, and Alan Arkin

WAIT UNTIL DARK   With Richard Crenna

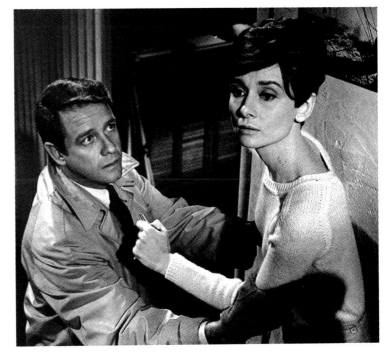

a superior performance. Aided by the generally strong script, she conveys superbly the combination of help-lessness and sense acuity sometimes found in the blind. Richard Crenna and Jack Weston give very fine shadings to diverse criminal characters. Alan Arkin uses a few unnecessary disguises and although a bit unrestrained, projects the appropriate sadistic

WAIT UNTIL DARK   With Alan Arkin

199

whole audience scream at once. The trick works perfectly. The screech from my audience was deafening."

—Hollis Alpert, *Saturday Review*

"Valiant is the name of Audrey through all this. Miss Hepburn's performance is appealing and expert, with as much humor and grace as anyone could bring to bear on the barely sufferable dialogue."

—*Newsweek*

"If you're not hooked by the well-oiled plot mechanics, you may just see the machinery of a plodding tale of a trio of thugs torturing a lovely blind lady, but if you are grabbed by the vulnerability of charming Audrey Hepburn, as child-woman as ever, and by the utter villainy of Alan Arkin—you will wind up screaming in the dark, which is what it's all about."

—Judith Crist, *TV Guide*

"*Wait Until Dark* is a moderately entertaining, impossibly contrived suspense movie. The plot complications, as the thing progresses, are wildly elaborate and rarely believable. The climax of this film is harrowing, directed by Terence Young with fine Hitchcockian intensity. Except for a slick introduction and three or four gruesome deaths that the camera relishes sadistically, it has not been 'opened up' beyond its single set—which was probably a wise decision for a work whose tension depends on intimacy.

"Audrey Hepburn overdoes her cute, artificial vocal mannerisms in the film's early scenes, but she's good in her more hysterical moments. Alan Arkin, cleverly cast against type as the evil, soft-spoken archvillain, can't help stealing the picture. Dripping with casual Brooklynese menace, it's a bit too much of a virtuoso performance to really convince you, but then given the exaggerated nature of the whole business, I was grateful for such stylish, winsome theatricality."

—Stephen Farber, *Film Quarterly*

WAIT UNTIL DARK Susy holds the doll that everyone wants

overtones. Director Young's achievement is aided by just-right nervous energy in Charles Lang's fluid camera. Henry Mancini's excellent score, which is deceptively simple, conveys the underlying drama via a dissonant bass. The obligatory title song, mercifully held for the end-titles, may be dismissed, forgiven and forgotten."

—"Murf," *Variety*

"The play worked well on the stage, and its artifices adapt smoothly to film. It should be mentioned that there is one final horrendous moment to make the

Robin and Marian

As Maid Marian in *Robin and Marian* (1976)

CAST

Sean Connery (*Robin Hood*); Audrey Hepburn (*Maid Marian/Mother Jennet*); Robert Shaw (*Sheriff of Nottingham*); Richard Harris (*King Richard*); Nicol Williamson (*Little John*); Denholm Elliott (*Will Scarlett*); Kenneth Haigh (*Sir Ranulf de Pudsey*); Ronnie Barker (*Friar Tuck*); Ian Holm (*King John*); Bill Maynard (*Mercadier*); Esmond Knight (*Old Defender*); Veronica Quilligan (*Sister Mary*); Peter Butterworth (*Surgeon*); John Barrett (*Jack*); Kenneth Cranham (*Jack's Apprentice*); Victoria Merida Roja (*Queen Isabella*); Montserrat Julio (*First Sister*); Victoria Hernandez Sanguino (*Second Sister*); Margarita Minguillon (*Third Sister*).

CREDITS

Director: Richard Lester; *Executive Producer*: Richard Shepherd; *Producer*: Denis O'Dell; *Screenwriter*: James Goldman; *Technicolor Cinematographer*: David Watkin; *Second-Unit Photography*: Paul Wilson; *Editor*: John Victor Smith; *Production Designer*: Michael Stringer; *Art Director*: Gil Parrondo; *Special Effects*: Eddie Fowlie; *Costumes*: Yvonne Blake; *Running time*: 106 minutes. Available on videocassette.

ORIGINAL RELEASE

1976; a Columbia Pictures release of a Rastar production.

THE FILM

When *Robin and Marian* was released in March of 1976, Audrey Hepburn had been away from the screen for eight and a half years, despite the efforts of producers and directors to lure her back in such vehicles as *Nicholas and Alexandra*, *Forty Carats*, *Conversation Piece*, and *A Bridge Too Far*. Naturally, many members of the international press chose to label this film Hepburn's "comeback." But she contested the term: "How can it be a comeback when I never really left? I had no intention of staying away so long." And she explained that she had chosen to put her husband and children first, working only when and if projects were agreeable and could be done without disrupting her family life.

Because *Robin and Marian* (originally known by such inadvisable titles as *The Death of Robin Hood* and *The Ballad of Robin and Marian*) was filmed in Spain, during a mere thirty-six days in the summer of 1975, the actress was able to visit with her family, as well as have impressionable sons Sean and Luca on location with her. They were particularly impressed that her costar was James Bond himself, Sean Connery.

A major factor in Hepburn's acceptance of this project was James Goldman's witty, original screenplay, which cast her as a woman of her own age (late forties), to say nothing of the opportunity of working with Connery, who had outlived his earlier 007 image to win critical praise and further audience popularity.

Richard Lester, who had directed the Beatles in *Help!* and *A Hard Day's Night*, as well as a rollicking remake of *The Three Musketeers*, recalled, "We arranged the shooting to accommodate her younger son's school holidays, which was very important to her because she was concerned that she spend as much time with him as possible." Reflecting the requirements of the movie's modest budget, Lester added, "She had been accustomed to being dressed by Givenchy, and she had one costume in the picture made out of oven-glove material, so it must have been a terrible shock to her to think, after eight years away from the screen, 'Is this what the world of film has come to?' She took it with immense good grace."

A sort of tragicomedy/adventure film, *Robin and Marian* picks up the Robin Hood legend some twenty years after most versions of the story, with Robin and his sidekick Little John returning to their old Sherwood Forest haunts world-weary from the Crusades and their sickening brutality. They're informed by former cohorts Friar Tuck and Will Scarlett that Maid Marian now lives at the nearby priory, where she has become the abbess. Marian greets Robin's return with mixed feelings, but after he rescues her from his longtime enemy, the Sheriff of Nottingham, who tries to arrest her on religious grounds, the two become lovers once again. Eventually, Robin and the Sheriff square off against one another in mortal combat, and Robin kills his adversary, but suffers a terrible wound himself. Marian nurses him at the abbey, but, knowing that he's doomed, she secretly poisons his wine, which she shares with him. Realizing what she's done, an incredulous Robin asks her why: Marian replies that it is because she loves him more than he'll ever know—"even more than God."

Working with fast-paced Richard Lester proved a revelation to Audrey Hepburn, who was used to the more leisurely style of the older Hollywood directors, who usually took at least three months to shoot a picture. During one postfilming interview, she described Lester as "fast and unencumbered by ego or dramatics; he is a whizbang with his many cameras and single takes." But she neglected to detail Lester's refusal to allow the retakes to which she was accustomed, and she wasn't quite ready for some of the rough location action, resulting in her having been thrown off a horse-drawn cart and dunked in a river by mistake—an accident that the director included in the film's final print. And Hepburn added, "I don't think Lester gave me enough time to do the love scenes with Sean Connery. I felt a bit rushed. And why did they have to show those rotten apples at the end? Were they supposed to represent Sean and me? I could've done without that last close-up of fruit turning rotten."

CRITICS' CIRCLE

"What prevents the movie from really losing its way are the performances of Sean Connery and Audrey Hepburn. They glow. They really do seem in love. And they make their feelings clear. This is a movie about the end of youth and high romance, about death and the possibility of simple human compassion. The passage of twenty years has given them grace and wisdom."

—Roger Ebert, *Chicago Sun-Times*

"Being a mixture of adventure, spectacle, gag comedy, drawing-room comedy and romance, *Robin and Marian* is even more of a confusion of inspirations than Mr. Goldman's *The Lion in Winter*, which was first of all a tightly constructed play. Yet *Robin and*

ROBIN AND MARIAN   Maid Marian as Mother Jennet

Marian is ultimately most appealing as a story of mismatched lovers who found too little too late.

"Neither Miss Hepburn nor Mr. Connery is actually ready for a geriatric ward yet, but their screen presences—the intensity of the images they project—are such that we are convinced that their late-August love is important and final, something that I'm not sure Mr. Lester knows how to cope with. The director is more comfortable debunking old myths than he is implementing new ones, yet the last section of *Robin and Marian* is virtually the stuff of grand opera. That it succeeds is remarkable, and in succeeding, it makes the glib manner of a lot of the earlier business almost intolerable.

"*Robin and Marian* is a hybrid movie, one that seems embarrassed by its feelings; yet it works best when it admits to those feelings, when it plays them straight."

—Vincent Canby, *New York Times*

WAIT UNTIL DARK   With Sean Connery

"I, for one, feel as if I've been robbed. *Robin and Marian* is a movie that seemed to have so much to offer. Most exciting of all, it was to be the film that marked Audrey Hepburn's return to the screen after much too long a time. It is nice to be able to report that Hepburn (except for the inevitable lines around the eyes) has changed very little, but it is also a pity that her enormous charm is wasted on such an impossible role; one doesn't believe the character of Marian for a minute, especially when she manages to turn up in a sparkling clean habit, wearing eye make-up and a pale lipstick, after days of camping out in Sherwood Forest."

—Kathleen Carroll, *New York Daily News*

"*Robin and Marian* is the latest exploration of a romantic past by Richard Lester, the gifted American director who does practically everything in Europe. On this trip he has taken a congenial, bittersweet story, a moody yet adventurous attitude, and a couple of splendid stars named Sean Connery and Audrey Hepburn. Though this is one of Lester's more successful films, it might have hit still higher peaks were it not for the lackluster screenplay by James Goldman—

A 1976 portrait

often smart-alecky, sometimes clever, but almost never wise. *Robin and Marian* is a picturebook movie that works almost entirely on a visual level, even though most scenes are jammed with words.

"Connery looks just great as our aging Robin. It's the kind of mildly macho part that suits him well these days, a far cry from the sham heroics of *Zardoz* or the vanished days of James Bond. Miss Hepburn has kept up her panache nicely during her years of vacation, and Lester's mild handling of her role allows her qualities to shine forth gently and tastefully."

—David Sterritt, *Christian Science Monitor*

"The great pity is that the cast assembled might have brought great vitality to a story like this. We have all seen recent evidence of the talents and power of such actors as Sean Connery, Robert Shaw and Nicol Williamson to regret the listless chores they have been given here. It has been all too long since we have seen Audrey Hepburn, possibly the only woman around who could make nun's habits look adorable. But it seems a cruel joke to have waited eight years to watch her do such dreary stuff. The idea of an antiheroic *Robin Hood* seems right for our times, but antiheroic should really mean more than lugubrious and flaccid."

—Howard Kissel, *Women's Wear Daily*

"Connery has become peculiarly adept at playing rugged, restless period adventurers; Audrey Hepburn's screen comeback is refreshingly dignified, and Nicol Williamson makes a particularly fine (and surprisingly restrained) Little John, dotingly fond of his master. But acting can only partially redeem the weaknesses of a script burdened with sagging dramatic tension and fuzzy characterizations—especially as the director himself provides insufficient support."

—Geoff Brown, *Monthly Film Bulletin*

"*Robin and Marian*, Richard Lester's new, twilight-hued film, is a ravishing romance about aging and death. But it's not about the autumnal years of mere mortals; this is a film about legends, and legends become even more beautiful with age. That's why, though *Robin and Marian* is haunted by ghosts and feelings of loss, its ultimate effect is so tonic. The movie reminds us that legends never die—that they are, instead, perpetually reborn.

"Miss Hepburn's new solidity and range serve her Maid Marian well. Connery, in Robin Hood, has found the payoff role to cap his characterizations in *The Wind and the Lion* and *The Man Who Would Be King* last year. *Robin and Marian* is the first fully realized Richard Lester picture since *Petulia* in 1968."

—Frank Rich, *New York Post*

"*Robin and Marian* is a grand and enthralling romantic saga in which everything jells gloriously and artistically, uplifting the spirits and replenishing the soul. It's what we grew up loving about movies, and Audrey Hepburn is one of the reasons we keep going, and loving them."

—Rex Reed, *New York Daily News*

As Elizabeth Roffe in *Sidney Sheldon's Bloodline* (1979)

Sidney Sheldon's Bloodline

(BLOODLINE)

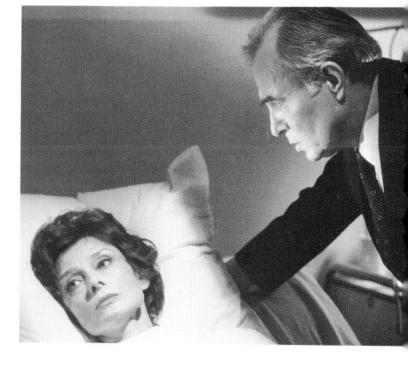

With James Mason in
Sidney Sheldon's Bloodline
(1979)

CAST

Audrey Hepburn (*Elizabeth Roffe*); Ben Gazzara (*Rhys Williams*); James Mason (*Sir Alec Nichols*); Claudia Mori (*Donatella*); Irene Papas (*Simonetta Palazzi*); Michelle Phillips (*Vivian Nichols*); Maurice Ronet (*Charles Martin*); Romy Schneider (*Helene Martin*); Omar Sharif (*Ivo Palazzi*); Beatrice Straight (*Kate Erling*); Gert Fröbe (*Inspector Max Hornung*); Wolfgang Preiss (*Julius Prager*); Marcel Bozzuffi (*Man in Black*); Pinkas Braun (*Dr. Wal*); Wulf Kessler (*Young Sam Roffe*); Maurice Colbourne (*Jon Swinton*); Guy Rolfe (*Tod Michaels*); Dietlinde Turban (*Terenia*); Walter Kohut (*Krauss*); Donald Symington (*Henley*); Charles Millot (*Inspector Bloche*); Ivan Desny (*Jeweller*); Vadim Glowna (*Dr. Joeppli*); Hans von Borsody (*Peasant Guard*); Derrick Branche (*Chemin-de-fer Player*); Josef Frölich (*Interpol Officer*); Klaus Guth (*Coroner*); Dale Van Husen (*Cameraman*); Friedrich von Ledebur (*Innkeeper*); Leslie Sands (*Doctor*); Lisa Woska (*Mrs. Wal*); Franziska Stömmer (*Innkeeper*); Yves Barsacq (*Bookseller*).

CREDITS

Director: Terence Young; *Producers*: David V. Picker and Sidney Beckerman; *Associate Producer*: Richard McWhorter; *Screenwriter*: Laird Koenig; *Based on the novel by* Sidney Sheldon; *Movielab Color Cinematog-*

rapher: Freddie Young; *Second-Unit Photography*: Cesare Allioni and Alexander Barbey; *Editor*: Ed Molin; *Production Designer*: Ted Haworth; *Art Directors*: Robert Cartwright, Savin Couelle, F. Dieter Bartels, Maxi Hareiter, and Helmut Gassner; *Set Decorators*: Hugh Scaife, Robert Christides, and Herta Pischinger; *Special Effects*: Richard Richtsfeld; *Music*: Ennio Morricone; *Costumes*: Enrico Sabbatini and Hubert de Givenchy; *Running time*: 116 minutes. Available on videocassette.

ORIGINAL RELEASE
1979; a Paramount release of a Geria production.

THE FILM
After a three-year hiatus—during which there was talk about Audrey Hepburn teaming with the long-absent Grace Kelly, as former ballet rivals, in *The Turning Point* (eventually filmed with Anne Bancroft and Shirley MacLaine), she followed up her "comeback" Maid Marian role with this commercially oriented project. Bestselling novelist Sidney Sheldon hadn't been happy with the 1977 movie version of his *The Other Side of Midnight*. But, with his friend, producer Sidney Beckerman, the instrumental force behind a screen adaptation of Sheldon's potboiler *Bloodline*, deals were set up involving the West German tax-shelter consortium, Geria, as well as the ABC television network, which would subsequently air the picture, three years after its theatrical run. Engaging Hepburn, at a salary of $1.25 million against 10 percent of the gross, ensured universal appeal for the project. And that casting paved the way for a colorful ensemble that blended the American with the European, attracting such international names as James Mason, Ben Gazzara, Irene Papas, Romy Schneider, Omar Sharif, Gert Frobe, and Beatrice Straight.

Hepburn was initially reluctant to accept the role of a twenty-three-year-old cosmetics heiress whose father is murdered, with herself becoming the next target of an unknown killer amid the continental jet set. But her *Wait Until Dark* director, Terence Young—already signed for the film—waged a persuasive get-Audrey campaign that eventually broke down her defenses. Altering the character's age to thirty-five helped convince the nearly fifty-year-old actress (who still looked a good decade younger). Although the results marked a new low point in the Hepburn

career, this could not be foreseen at the start of the production. And if much of the resultant movie is confusing and difficult to follow, editing may have been largely responsible; when ABC aired *Bloodline* in September 1982, the 116-minute film was given a three-hour time slot. In so doing, some 12 minutes of censorable material were cut, while 37 minutes of footage never seen in movie theaters were added. Thus, for better or worse, those who managed to tape the network version may be better able to make sense of *Bloodline* than those who view the 116-minute theatrical-release edition now available on videocassette.

CRITICS' CIRCLE
"*Sidney Sheldon's Bloodline*, based on the recent Sheldon novel that sold well, is both better and worse than the film version of Sidney Sheldon's *The Other Side of Midnight*, which was apparently made before Mr. Sheldon's agent had the clout to squeeze the Sheldon name into the title. *Bloodline* has a more attractive, more able cast, and it has a lot more scenery, but it seems constructed entirely of loose ends and superfluous information. *The Other Side of Midnight* was the undisputed junk-movie of the year, but it made a certain amount of narrative sense. *Bloodline* doesn't. As he demonstrated in his James Bond films, Terence Young is a director of some comic style, but though *Bloodline* is often laughable, it has no sense of humor. *Bloodline* takes Miss Hepburn's Givenchy clothes more seriously than it does the actress who wears them, not always becomingly. Under these circumstances, there's no reason to comment on the quality of the individual performances."

—Vincent Canby, *New York Times*

"Using an inordinate amount of very high-key lighting and occasional filters, Freddie Young's camera mostly stays at a respectable distance from Audrey Hepburn, whose prim, unflamboyant character sets exceedingly narrow emotional parameters for the story. Though it would take several pictures on the level of *Bloodline* to seriously damage her stature, it's a shame she picks something like this now that she works so seldom."

—"Cart.," *Variety*

"*Sidney Sheldon's Bloodline*—that's the official title—offers the chance to see Audrey Hepburn on the screen again but under what rotten circumstances! The movie is claptrap, a murder mystery with no suspense, although Ennio Morricone's music, sounding like something written for *The Old Dark House*, tries desperately to make us think there is. Looking constrained and physically drawn, Hepburn seems to be on screen simply as a model for her Givenchy wardrobe. As a team, she and Ben Gazzara evoke no spark, no charisma. *The Other Side of Midnight*, the previous movie from a Sheldon novel, at least was diverting with its solemnly campy approach to the high-style, jet-set life of its characters. *Bloodline* is ponderous and vacant."

—Ernest Leogrande, *New York Daily News*

"It is all unutterably chic, inexpressibly absurd, and saved from being painfully tedious only by a personable cast doing their damndest."

—Tom Milne, *Monthly Film Bulletin*

"Everyone enjoys sitting down with a good trashy novel now and then, something to read and not disturb the grey matter. But when trashy becomes trash, as

in *Bloodline*, it's time to beware. The script by Laird Koenig is one step below soap opera and has acting to match. Only Gert Fröbe as the German police inspector with a passion for computers transcends this. The mind boggles that such a film could be so dreadful, even when in the hands of Terence Young, a director of some style who put the oomph into the first three James Bond films. One could go to see *Bloodline* to see the de Givenchy gowns Audrey Hepburn wears, or to see the lovely scenery of New York, London, Paris, Sardinia, Rome and Munich. There's even a lilting theme by Ennio Morricone that is quite pleasant the first 100 times around. Otherwise, it's a trying two hours. The softcore scenes that are responsible for the R rating make the movie totally unsuitable for kids. And the film's quality makes it totally unsuitable for anyone else."

—Paul Hyman, *Boxoffice*

"If I were Sidney Sheldon, I'd demand to have my name removed from the title of this torpid turkey."

—*Newsweek*

"Audrey Hepburn's appearances on the screen are so few and so far between that I wish she wouldn't waste them. Now she turns up in *Bloodline*, a titanic turkey that provides sleepless nights for Hepburn and her fans. It's really *Sidney Sheldon's Bloodline*, to get the title accurate, and he's welcome to it.

"Filmed in five countries with lush photography by Freddie *Lawrence of Arabia* Young, fashion-magazine sets, a glamorous cast and $22 million to play with, it's really mind-boggling that *Sidney Sheldon's Bloodline* makes so little sense and remains so boring in the process. At fifty, Audrey Hepburn is still vulnerable and doe-like, the perfect victim in Givenchy clothes. She works well with director Terence Young, who performed the same chore on her last Hollywood film, *Wait Until Dark*. But this time out, they all seem tired."

—Rex Reed, *New York Daily News*

SIDNEY SHELDON'S BLOODLINE   With James Mason

They All Laughed

THEY ALL LAUGHED   With Ben Gazzara

CAST

Audrey Hepburn (*Angela Niotes*); Ben Gazzara (*John Russo*); John Ritter (*Charles Rutledge*); Colleen Camp (*Christy Miller*); Patti Hansen (*Deborah "Sam" Wilson*); Dorothy Stratten (*Dolores Martin*); George Morfogen (*Leon Leondopolous*); Blaine Novak (*Arthur Brodsky*); Sean Ferrer (*José*); Linda MacEwen (*Amy Lester*); Lisa Dunsheath (*Tulips*); Sheila Stodden (*Barbara-Jo*); Joyce Hyser (*Sylvia*); Elizabeth Peña (*Rita*); Shawn Casey (*Laura*); Vassily Lambrinos (*Stavros Niotes*); Glenn Scarpelli (*Michael Niotes*); Antonia Bogdanovich (*Stefania Russo*); Alexandra Bogdanovich (*Georgina Russo*); Riccardo Bertoni (*Mr. Martin*).

CREDITS

Director-Screenwriter: Peter Bogdanovich; *Executive Producer*: Mike Moder; *Producers*: George Morfogen and Blaine Novak; *Associate Producer*: Russell Schwartz; *Movielab Color Cinematographer*: Robby Müller; *Editors*: Scott Vickrey and William Carruth; *Art Director*: Kert Lundell; *Music Coordinator*: Douglas Dilge; *Costumes*: Peggy Farrell; *Running time*: 115 minutes. Available on videocassette and laser disc.

ORIGINAL RELEASE

1981; a Moon Pictures release of a Time-Life production.

THE FILM

Produced in the first half of 1980, *They All Laughed* suffered a problematic history. When the finished product failed to please Twentieth Century Fox, which planned to distribute it, director Peter Bogdanovich was obliged to buy it back from the studio and release it himself, which he did under the banner "Moon Pictures." At the same time, he had to come to terms with the murder, by her jealous husband, of his mistress—and one of the picture's stars—Dorothy Stratten. Making a bad situation worse, Stratten's role in the film mirrored all too closely her real life plight. Although Audrey Hepburn is top-billed, hers is actually a supporting part. But having her aboard helped Bogdanovich get the movie made—especially since it also featured the star of that director's *Saint Jack*, Ben Gazzara, with whom Hepburn had reportedly been emotionally involved during the making of *Bloodline*.

In June 1980, *New York Daily News* columnist "Suzy" reported that during the filming of *They All*

Laughed, there had been "some great tension on the set between them, especially during the love scenes—even some downright hostility." Hepburn's son, Sean Ferrer, was also in the cast in a few short scenes as Stratten's lover. Shot in New York City on a modest budget, this antic comedy about a trio of Big Apple detectives and their romantic pursuits failed to attract much box-office attention, even as the final film of murdered *Playboy* Playmate Stratten.

CRITICS' CIRCLE

They All Laughed is gorgeous fun. . . .

"Rarely does a film come along featuring such an extensive array of attractive characters with whom it is simply a pleasure to spend two hours. Nothing of great importance happens in a strict plot sense, but this *La Ronde*–like tale is intensely devoted to the sexual and amorous sparks struck among some unusually magnetic people, all within a PG framework respectful of the traditions of classical cinema.

"Hepburn doesn't have a line to speak for the entire first hour (much of the film is devoted to vaguely voyeuristic pursuit and observation on the part of the detectives), but ultimately she emerges winningly as the most mature and discreet character in the group."

—"Cart.," *Variety*

"Warm and graceful, Peter Bogdanovich's *They All Laughed* is one of the better films so far this season. With nary a word of verbal exposition, producer-writer-director Bogdanovich keeps this story—of a New York detective agency specializing (it appears) in tailing spouses suspected of adultery—moving at a breakneck pace.

Robby Müller's Manhattan photography glows, as do the performers. Chief among them is John Ritter, who plays pretty much the same character as he does on *Three's Company*, but with less wisecracking and more klutziness; the result is a sympathetic and vulnerable portrayal. Colleen Camp gives one of the most unique and funny performances around as a fast-talking, marginally successful country rock singer. Shown to less advantage are the film's main star attractions: Ben Gazzara and Audrey Hepburn. As the oldest and wisest of the detectives, Gazzara smirks through all his scenes, probably wondering why his character is not given more to do than snuggle up to his daughters or cast fond and teary gazes at the lovely Hepburn. Her role suffers, too, from malnutrition, and the scenes of the two of them alone together are the film's only slow moments. In the end, though, all shortcomings can be forgotten, due to the presence of Dorothy Stratten. As a fun-loving, girlish beauty who comes home every night to a suspicious, jealous and potentially violent husband, the parallels with the actress's senseless death become eerie and poignant."

—Gerry Putzer, *Hollywood Reporter*

"The title is *They All Laughed*. Would that anyone could laugh. The film, which is meant to be a witty, liberated sex comedy, was directed by Peter Bogdanovich from his own, apparently still unfinished screenplay. Any way you look at it—as a comedy, as moviemaking, as a financial investment—*They All Laughed* is an immodest disaster. It's aggressive in its ineptitude. It grates on the nerves like a 78 rpm record played at 33 rpm. *They All Laughed* has a number of attractive people in it, some less badly used than others. Appearing to something less than good advantage are John Ritter, whose role is a variation on the clumsy, bespectacled square played by Ryan O'Neal in the director's much classier *What's Up, Doc?*, and the elegant Audrey Hepburn, whom Mr. Bogdanovich treats so shabbily that if this were a marriage instead of a movie, she'd have grounds for immediate divorce. Miss Hepburn looks game and is well, if casually, dressed as a rich Italian industrialist's bored wife who, inexplicably, falls in love with the cloddish private eye assigned to trail her. This fellow is played by Ben Gazzara in the way of someone who labors under the misapprehension that he is loaded with charm, nothing less than a combination of Bogart, Grant and Gable. However, Mr. Gazzara can't even smile convincingly in the many close-ups Mr. Bogdanovich has given him, perhaps in lieu of a character to act.

"The only thing that *They All Laughed* does is certify Mr. Bogdanovich's good taste in beautiful women."

—Vincent Canby, *New York Times*

"Peter Bogdanovich's screwball comedy *They All Laughed* was made for about the same amount of money Paramount Pictures, Milos Forman and Dino de Laurentiis spent for ginger ale on *Ragtime*. Yet it is fresher, funnier, and much more entertaining. Not

THEY ALL LAUGHED   As Angela Niotes

only is it named after a Gershwin song, but it has a ditzy, frazzled rhythm of its own. I loved the way these people were so casual and cheerful about their interchangeable sexual liaisons, and I loved the way their attitudes and life styles exemplified the boil and perk and bounce of contemporary New Yorkers. Their roles, like the film, have no conventional structure, but that's okay because the whole point is to make you feel like you're out on the town with the guys. They work for something called the Odyssey Detective Agency, where the motto is 'We Never Sleep,' and everyone in the movie is busy night and day living up to it.

"What the elegant, structured Audrey Hepburn is doing in the middle of all this lunacy is a bigger mystery than anything the horny, off-the-wall detectives ever have to solve, but she fits in nicely and seems to be having a ball. So did I. So will you."

–Rex Reed, *New York Daily News*

"Despite the top-billing of Hepburn and Gazzara along with Ritter, *They All Laughed* is very much an ensemble piece. Whether 'they laughed' because some of them were happy or horny or stoned or embarrassed, it seems they were *all* glad to be alive and together (and in New York), and Bogdanovich gets that point across marvelously. The positive side of New York City has seldom before been so splendidly photographed or the town been made to seem such a madcap carnival."

—"J. P.," *Film Journal*

"At 52, Hepburn, the eternal gamine, has become a figure of icy chic; the lilt in her voice now has the gravity of years. But she is still a radiant presence, and she blesses the end of *They All Laughed* with a display of poignant maturity. One would gladly pay to hear her read the Bel Air phone book. One would not be surprised to know that was Bogdanovich's next project."

—*Time*

Directed by William Wyler

CREDITS

Director/Editor: Aviva Slesin; *Executive Producer*: Catherine Wyler; *Producer*: Catherine Tatge; *Narration and Interviews*: A. Scott Berg; *Running time*: 58 minutes.

THE FILM

An excellent documentary on the film director William Wyler (1902–81), this feature was conceived by his daughter, Catherine, as a loving tribute to him. First shown at the World Film Festival in Montreal in the summer of 1986, it was subsequently offered at that year's New York Film Festival, among other specialized engagements. In 1987, PBS stations presented it on television as part of its "American Masters" summer series. Utilizing a wealth of film clips, many in black and white, the movie features interviews with Bette Davis, Samantha Eggar, Greer Garson, Lillian Hellman, Audrey Hepburn, Charlton Heston, John Huston, Laurence Olivier, Gregory Peck, Ralph Richardson, Terence Stamp, Barbra Streisand, Billy Wilder, Talli (the former Margaret Tallichet) Wyler, and the director himself. Among the honors garnered by *Directed by William Wyler* are the 1986 Cine Golden Eagle Award and the 1987 Chicago Festival Gold Hugo Award.

William Wyler directed Audrey Hepburn in three diverse films: *Roman Holiday*, *The Children's Hour*, and *How to Steal a Million*.

ORIGINAL RELEASE

1986; a Tatge production.

CRITICS' CIRCLE

"A first-rate Hollywood retrospective often is as good as the movies it chronicles. Here's one—a documentary about William Wyler and his films. Entertaining and informative, it's also a trove of delightful trivia. Some of the best of the Hollywood talk comes from Wyler himself, interviewed only a few days before he died in 1981. The documentary brings fresh perspective, not just to the director, but to old Hollywood as well."

–Leo Seligsohn, *New York Newsday*

"A thorough and an unusually informative reminiscence of Wyler's films and work habits. His directorial tyranny, described by Audrey Hepburn and others, is now recalled fondly, like old veterans recalling stories of a tough drill instructor. If you're a film buff,

Directed by William Wyler offers behind-the-scene nuggets that are priceless."

—David Bianculli, *New York Post*

"In *Directed by William Wyler*, a brisk, funny and heartfelt tribute to this inarguably great filmmaker, many of the actors who worked with Wyler rattle off their cherished horror stories, mostly of having to go through take after take of a scene until the master was satisfied. 'He made me do 48 takes in front of 250 extras,' sputters Bette Davis of her servitude in *Jezebel*. But what also becomes clear from the one-hour documentary is the genuine respect and affection those same actors felt for Wyler. 'Actors fought to work with Willie,' says Gregory Peck, who made *Roman Holiday* with him. But the most valuable commentary comes from Wyler himself. He seems wiry, blunt and refreshingly unsentimental, as is this film. There is none of the usual rhapsodic gush that one encounters at tributes and award shows. We are not being lectured to about Wyler's greatness, but it comes through brilliantly nevertheless."

—Tom Shales, *Washington Post*

"*Directed by William Wyler* is full of informed admiration. Miss Hellman remembers emerging in tears from an advance screening of *Mrs. Miniver*, Wyler's thinly disguised but hugely successful World War II propaganda film. When he asked the playwright why she was crying, she says she told him: 'Because it's such a piece of junk, Willie. It's so far beneath you.'

"Lord Olivier remembers how Wyler insulted him during the shooting of *Wuthering Heights*, and Miss Hepburn how he scared her into tears on the set of *Roman Holiday*. Yet each performer testifies to Wyler's miraculous way of getting the best from every actor he worked with."

—Vincent Canby, *New York Times*

DIRECTED BY WILLIAM WYLER   On location with Wyler in Rome for *Roman Holiday*

Love Among Thieves

LOVE AMONG THIEVES   With Robert Wagner

CAST

Audrey Hepburn (*Baroness Caroline DuLac*); Robert Wagner (*Mike Chambers*); Jerry Orbach (*Spicer*); Patrick Bauchau (*Alan Channing*); Samantha Eggar (*Solange DuLac*); Brion James (*Andre*); Christopher Neame (*Ian*); Ismael "East" Carlo (*Mazo*); Alma Beltran (*Airline Clerk*); John Chandler (*Hotel Clerk*).

CREDITS

Director: Roger Young; *Executive Producer*: Karen Mack; *Producer*: Robert A. Papazian; *Associate Producer*: Stephanie Austin; *Screenwriters*: Stephen Black and Henry Stern; *Color Cinematographer*: Gayne Rescher; *Editor*: James Mitchell; *Production Designer*: Peter Wooley; *Miss Hepburn's Costumes*: Hubert de Givenchy; *Music*: Arthur B. Rubinstein; *Running time*: 100 minutes.

ORIGINAL RELEASE

1987; Robert Papazian Productions/ABC Television.

THE FILM

Six years after her last theatrical feature, *They All Laughed*, Audrey Hepburn proved a welcome sight for television audiences when she teamed with Robert Wagner for a venture variously titled *Kind of a Lady* and *Here a Thief, There a Thief* prior to its February 1989 airing as *Love Among Thieves*. Hopes were high for what sounded in advance like a lighthearted Hitchcock-style mixture of comedy, mystery, and, judging by the title, romance. As of old, Hepburn's gowns were designed by Givenchy, but this time all of the production was shot in twenty-two days in the Western U.S., with locations ranging from San Francisco and Southern California locales to Tucson. Obviously ignorant of 1957's *Mayerling* and her other television appearances from the fifties, ABC publicists promoted this as Audrey Hepburn's TV debut!

CRITICS' CIRCLE

"Jewel thieves and intrigue were not unknown commodities in the entertainment business. And in ABC's

215

telefilm *Love Among Thieves*, these twin entities receive some fine new facets and polishing, given a fanciful high-gloss treatment. Audrey Hepburn stars as Baroness Caroline DuLac, a world renowned concert pianist turned Fabergé egg napper, befriended by a rough-and-tumble bearded fellow named Mike Chambers, played by Robert Wagner. Before assumptions are made impugning Ms. DuLac's character, let me say that the impetus for her Fabergé snatching is triggered by the kidnapping of her fiancé (Patrick Bauchau), who is being held for the high-stakes eggs. Into this equation toss a shadowy stalker referred to as Spicer (Jerry Orbach).

"Stylized swooping swings is how *Thieves* operates. Moreover, the lovely and lanky-limbed Hepburn is great fun to watch, a gal who knows how to get the most out of her action-adventure. And Wagner as her opportune knight-errant has a humdinger of a star turn, obviously enjoying himself this TV trip-out. *Love Among Thieves* is a surefire, sassy yarn that succeeds as envigorating entertainment."

Miles Beller, *Hollywood Reporter*

"Stooping way down to conquer, delectable Audrey Hepburn, making her telefilm bow, finds herself somewhere between car chases and slapdash plotting that's seen far better days. With its irrelevant title, *Love Among Thieves* pants for fresh air. Roger Young has directed the expedition with silly sight gags and inconsequential exchanges for the two principals. Hepburn manages to get across the confusing character with some humor—one scream she tosses off earns a guffaw—and her discomfort with the renownd pianist's situations has a limited amusement. But viewers and Hepburn deserve better—by a long shot!"

—"Tone.," *Variety*

"You have to give Robert Wagner this much. He must be a genuine charmer to have enticed first Liz (*There Must Be a Pony*) Taylor and now Audrey Hepburn to co-star with him on the electronic screen. So what if both shows weren't worth the videotape they were recorded on. You still have to give the guy credit. Hepburn tries to play the same sort of sweetly sexy ingenue she was in *Charade*—twenty-four years later. She's a concert pianist in San Francisco who steals some Fabergé eggs because they've been demanded as ransom for her sleazy husband [*sic*]. Thus begin

LOVE AMONG THIEVES   As Caroline Dulac, in her Givenchy gown

chases across Mexico, chance encounters with Wagner and a very little romance in a story composed mainly of long, slow, sloppy build-ups to anticlimaxes. I still love Hepburn and, like her, I can't help being charmed by Wagner. That's what makes their show so sad."

—Jeff Jarvis, *People*

"Miss Hepburn, still lovely though even more fragile than usual, is introduced wearing a black Givenchy gown as Caroline DuLac, a baroness and concert

216

pianist. By the film's end, nobody except poor Caroline turns out to be who he or she is supposed to be. But at that point, few viewers are likely to care. Miss Hepburn, who has plodded through the rest of the picture in a single print dress with broad shoulders, does finally get to make an elegant exit in a red version of what appears to be her favorite Givenchy gown. She deserves several more in a range of colors for having to trudge through this turkey."

—John J. O'Connor, *New York Times*

"Playing opposite a bearded Wagner, Hepburn seems utterly at sea as a cultured pearl of a millionairess who falls in with coarse, leaden company. Part of the problem with this is that Hepburn, trying to convince us she can muck around, is trying to do too much. Her character is supposed to be a concert pianist who goes on a wild caper. When she's concertizing, we see Hepburn as we've become accustomed to her—dressed in Givenchy and performing with customary dignity. After she takes to the road in Mexico, where the awkward story line has her exchanging a ransom of bejeweled eggs for her kidnapped fiancé, she loses all that class and style. We can only cringe when we see Hepburn submit herself to this silliness. She's dragged down by bad writing and hack characterization. Her chemistry with Wagner—who tries to hide his shallow suavity behind a beard and a cloud of cigar smoke—is not particularly appealing or compelling.

"There certainly is the temptation for television to grab stars of Hepburn's reputation, then give them the hack treatment, thinking the audience will be hooked by the star without paying mind to the vehicle. In *Love Among Thieves*, we see an unfortunate kind of exploitation. There's Audrey Hepburn, the big name, in a rattletrap jalopy of a vehicle. Straining to be funny and cute, she is an embarrassment. And that's not her style."

—Monica Collins, *U.S.A. Today*

"Waltzing back into the affections of her fans . . . is that lissome, graceful and deliciously feminine actress, Audrey Hepburn, with only one message to deliver: entertainment.

"After so many issue films, I confess that *Love Among Thieves* is a welcome relief—though I would have wished for a better vehicle to mark the star's return. For example, it would have been nice to see her in a film that took advantage of her style and elegance, one which called for the kind of knockout outfits she wore in such films as *Breakfast at Tiffany's*, *Roman Holiday*, *My Fair Lady* and the stage production of *Gigi*. True, at the beginning and end of *Love Among Thieves* she is stunningly attired, but for most of the film she wears a red shirtwaist dress. All I can say is that it's a waste.

"Nevertheless, the actress hasn't lost her feel for a light, adventurous, romantic cinematic escapade. Slim and attractive, despite the added years, Hepburn still is the essence of poise and elegance, and can drift down a flight of stairs with the same grace she displayed in *Funny Face* with Fred Astaire. The lady is a charmer, and it's good to have her back."

—Kay Gardella, *New York Daily News*

"*Love Among Thieves* is an awful movie that makes the false assumption that Robert Wagner, Audrey Hepburn and three Fabergé eggs have enough allure to obscure the most spineless of scripts. An unfortunate travesty, especially considering the fact that it's Hepburn's TV movie debut."

—Ricardo Hunter Garcia, *New York Post*

Always

ALWAYS   With Richard Dreyfuss

CAST

Richard Dreyfuss (*Pete Sandich*); Holly Hunter (*Dorinda Durston*); Brad Johnson (*Ted Baker*); John Goodman (*Al Yackey*); Audrey Hepburn (*Hap*); Roberts Blossom (*Dave*); Keith David (*Powerhouse*); Ed Van Nuys (*Nails*); Marg Helgenberger (*Rachel*); Dale Dye (*Fire Boss*); Brian Haley (*Alex*); James Lashly (*Charlie*); Michael Steve Jones (*Grey*); Kim Robillard (*Air Traffic Controller*); Jim Sparkman (*Dispatcher*); Doug McGrath (*Bus Driver*).

CREDITS

Director: Steven Spielberg; *Producers*: Steven Spielberg, Frank Marshall, and Kathleen Kennedy; *Second-Unit Director*: Frank Marshall; *Screenwriters*: Jerry Belson and Diane Thomas; *Based on the screenplay A Guy Named Joe by* Dalton Trumbo; *Adaptation*: Frederick Hazlitt Brennan; *Story by* Chandler Sprague and David Boehm; *DeLuxe Color Cinematographer*: Mikael Salomon; *Additional Photography*: John Toll and Gary Graver; *Aerial Photography*: Frank Holgate and Alexander Witt; *Editor*: Michael Kahn; *Production Designer*: James Bissell; *Art Directors*: Chris Burian-Mohr, Richard Reynolds (Montana) and Richard Fernandez (Washington); *Set Decorators*: Jack Haye and Keith London; *Special Effects*: Mike Wood; *Forest Fire Special Effects*: Jeff Jarvis; *Costumes*: Ellen Mirojnick; *Music*: John Williams; *Running time*: 121 minutes. Available on videocassette and laser disc.

ORIGINAL RELEASE

1989; a Universal/United Artists release of an Amblin Entertainment production.

THE FILM

Steven Spielberg's sentimental remake of the 1943 Spencer Tracy–Irene Dunne–Van Johnson fantasy *A Guy Named Joe* retained much of that World War II story's basic structure, while changing the central character of a fighter pilot to an aerial firefighter. Richard Dreyfuss took over the Tracy role, with Holly Hunter and newcomer Brad Johnson in the costarring parts, as the earthbound romantic pair who discover a mutual attraction after Dreyfuss is killed in a plane crash. In her final motion picture, Audrey Hepburn received "Special Appearance by" billing as the 1989 counterpart of Lionel Barrymore's heavenly messenger, "The General," in the earlier movie. Was her supporting character, Hap, supposed to be an angel? In a 1989 interview, the actress said, "Nobody knows what I am, even Steven Spielberg. I would say I'm a spirit more than anything. But not an extraterrestrial. No, it's just plain old me with a sweater on."

Softening some of the negative impressions of Audrey Hepburn left by *Bloodline* and *They All Laughed*, at least *Always* afforded the actress a graceful last curtain call to her essentially great career.

CRITICS' CIRCLE

"*Always* is bigger and busier than *A Guy Named Joe* in every way. The film's occasional moments of sweetness—Audrey Hepburn appearing briefly as an angel gently alerting Pete (Richard Dreyfuss) to his new status—are too easily upstaged by clutter and silly, implausible gags. *Always* is extravagantly good-looking at times, but its visual style is more effective in recalling other films of Mr. Spielberg's than in complementing this particular story. The big, inviting blue skies and the golden light streaming through windows, even the oasis of daisies in a burned-out forest where Ms. Hepburn first appears, turn out to be powerfully distracting. Gentle and moving as it means to be, *Always* is overloaded. There is barely a scene here that wouldn't have worked better with less fanfare."

—Janet Maslin, *New York Times*

"The heavens part and angels' feathers scatter as daredevils buck the sky in *Always*, Steven Spielberg's sleepy update of a Spencer Tracy wartime fantasy. Boiling clouds and barrel-rolling aside, there's more drag than lift as this sweetly sluggish romantic adventure struggles to get airborne in the 1990s. One minute

ALWAYS   The film's main players: Richard Dreyfuss, Holly Hunter, and Brad Johnson

As Hap in *Always*
(1989)

With Richard Dreyfuss in
Always

220

Pete is rescuing his good friend Al (jolly John Goodman), the next he's getting a haircut, a ludicrous
introduction to the seraph Hap (Audrey Hepburn,
stern in a white cable-knit sweater). Babbling something about the breath of the gods, Hap tells Pete
that basically he's grounded, that he must inspire
another to greatness before ascending to higher
realms.

"Clearly, Spielberg wants to give us *It's a Wonderful
Life* with propellers. Alas, our spirits are not elevated
as they are and were in that redemptive perennial,

A portrait from the early 1990s

221

a story of one man's renewed faith in the value of his life."

—Rita Kempley, *Washington Post*

"Not every Steven Spielberg film can or should be a grandiose cinematic event. The kind of film he would have made if he had been a studio contract director during Hollywood's golden era, *Always* is a relatively small-scale, engagingly casual, somewhat silly, but always entertaining fantasy. The supernatural elements of *Always* may cause some tittering. In place of the fliers' heaven in *Joe*, with starchy commanding officer Lionel Barrymore giving Tracy a moving pep talk on his role in the war effort, Spielberg has nothing more to offer than a fey sylvan afterlife supervised by bromide-spouting Audrey Hepburn. She's alluring as always, but corny as a live-action fairy godmother.

"John Williams' music is rousing, and Spielberg wittily substitutes 'Smoke Gets in Your Eyes' for 'I'll Get By' as the couple's theme music. It's a shame that the haunting melody from Irving Berlin's 'Always,' which would have been so appropriate here, reportedly was denied to Spielberg."

—"Mac.," *Variety*

"Fighting forest fires in Montana doesn't translate into anything like World War II, and while there is a great bittersweetness in Richard Dreyfuss's longing for Holly Hunter after he dies, there is also great foolishness in Audrey Hepburn's embarrassing appearance as an angelic tour guide trying to steer Dreyfuss through the hereafter. The screenplay—

credited to Jerry (*Fun with Dick and Jane*) Belson—is mostly along the mega-sentimental lines of Hepburn's comment about the afterlife that 'The love we hold back is the only pain that follows us here.' There is too much serious-toned posthumous love story, not enough wit or perspective.

"In any case, it doesn't seem that the ghosts of Spencer Tracy, Victor Fleming, who directed *A Guy Named Joe*, or Dalton Trumbo, who wrote it, were hovering around Spielberg to offer much in the way of useful advice—unless they stayed away to keep Spielberg from getting more confused than he already is about the distinction between real life and life as seen in old movies."

—Ralph Novak, *People*

"Audrey Hepburn would probably be everybody's choice to play an angel, but Hepburn holding forth to the dead Pete in wheat field or sanctified clearings in a forest is no more interesting than any other actor required to twinkle."

—David Denby, *New York*

"In a cameo as the heavenly sage who sends Dreyfuss back to earth, Audrey Hepburn is incandescent. Her dialogue is treacle, but she sells it with an effortless grace that shows why she is still a legend at sixty. Hepburn's brief appearance can't fill the void in *Always*, but her movie-star magic demonstrates precisely what the rest of the film is missing."

—*Rolling Stone*

ALWAYS   As Hap

ORDER NOW! - Citadel Film & Television Books

If you like this book, you'll love Citadel Press's other television and movie books. A complete listing of these books appears below.

And if you know what books you want, why not order now? It's easy! **Just call 1-800-447-BOOK and have your MasterCard or Visa ready. (Tell the operator code #1598) Or use our toll-free sales fax 1-800-866-1966.**

FILM:
STARS
Al Pacino
Arnold Schwarzenegger
Audrey Hepburn
Barbra Streisand Films;
  Scrapbook
Bela Lugosi
Bette Davis
The Bowery Boys
Brigitte Bardot
Buster Keaton
Carole Lombard
Cary Grant
Charlie Chaplin
Clark Gable
Clint Eastwood
Curly
Dustin Hoffman
Edward G. Robinson
Elizabeth Taylor
Elvis Presley
The Elvis Scrapbook
Errol Flynn
Frank Sinatra
Gary Cooper
Gene Kelly
Gina Lollobrigida
Glenn Close
Gloria Swanson
Gregory Peck
Greta Garbo
Harrison Ford
Henry Fonda
Humphrey Bogart
Ingrid Bergman
Jack Lemmon
Jack Nicholson
James Cagney
James Dean: Behind the Scene
Jane Fonda
Jeanette MacDonald & Nelson
  Eddy
Joan Crawford
John Wayne Films; Reference
  Book; Scrapbook; Trivia Book
John Wayne's The Alamo
Judy Garland
Katharine Hepburn
Kirk Douglas
Laurel & Hardy

Lauren Bacall
Laurence Olivier
Mae West
Marilyn Monroe
Marlene Dietrich
Marlon Brando
Marx Brothers
Moe Howard & the Three
  Stooges
Olivia de Havilland
Orson Welles
Paul Newman
Peter Lorre
Rita Hayworth
Robert De Niro
Robert Redford
Sean Connery
Sexbomb: Jayne Mansfield
Shirley MacLaine
Shirley Temple
The Sinatra Scrapbook
Spencer Tracy
Steve McQueen
Three Stooges Scrapbook
Tom Hanks
Vincent Price
Warren Beatty
W.C. Fields
William Holden
William Powell
A Wonderful Life: James Stewart
DIRECTORS
Alfred Hitchcock
Cecil B. DeMille
Federico Fellini
Frank Capra
John Huston
Steven Spielberg
Woody Allen
GENRE
Black Hollywood, Vol. 1 & 2
Classic Foreign Films: From
  1960 to Today
Classic Gangster Films
Classic Science Fiction Films
Classics of the Horror Film
Cult Horror Films
Cult Science Fiction Films
Divine Images: Jesus on Screen
Early Classics of Foreign Film
Great Baseball Films

Great French Films
Great German Films
Great Italian Films
The Great War Films
Harry Warren & the Hollywood
  Musical
Hispanic Hollywood
Hollywood Bedlam: Screwball
  Comedies
The Hollywood Western
The Incredible World of 007
Jewish Image in American Film
The Lavender Screen: The Gay
  and Lesbian Films
Martial Arts Movies
Merchant Ivory Films
The Modern Horror Film
Money, Women & Guns: Crime
  Movies
More Classics of the Horror Film
Movie Psychos & Madmen
Our Huckleberry Friend: Johnny
  Mercer
Second Feature: "B" Films
They Sang! They Danced! They
  Romanced!
Thrillers
Words and Shadows: Literature
  on the Screen
DECADE
Classics of the Silent Screen
Films of the Twenties
Films of the Thirties
More Films of the '30s
Films of the Forties
Films of the Fifties
Lost Films of the '50s
Films of the Sixties
Films of the Seventies
Films of the Eighties
SPECIAL INTEREST
Bugsy (Illustrated screenplay)
The Citadel Treasury of Famous
  Movie Lines
Comic Support
The Critics Were Wrong
  (Misguided Movie Reviews)
Cutting Room Floor
Did She or Didn't She: Behind
  Bedroom Doors
Film Flubs

Film Flubs: The Sequel
Filmmaking on the Fringe
Final Curtain
First Films
Hollywood Cheesecake
Howard Hughes in Hollywood
How to Meet & Hang Out w/Stars
Jim Carrey Scrapbook
Lost Films
More Character People
Most Influential Women in Film
The Nightmare Never Ends:
  A Nightmare on Elm Street
100 Best Films of the Century
701 Toughest Movie Trivia
  Questions
Sex in Films
Sex In the Movies
Sherlock Holmes
Shot on this Site
Son of Film Flubs
Total Exposure: Nude Scenes
Who Is That?: Familiar Faces and
  Forgotten Names
Women's Book of Movie Quotes
The Worst Movies of All Time
"You Ain't Heard Nothin' Yet!"
TELEVISION:
America on the Rerun
The "Cheers" Trivia Book
Classic TV Westerns
Favorite Families of TV
Gilligan, Maynard & Me
Heather! (Locklear)
Mary, Mary, Maryl (Tyler
  Moore)
The Northern Exposure Book
The Official Andy Griffith Show
  Scrapbook
The 1001 Toughest TV Trivia
  Questions of All Time
The Quantum Leap Book
The "Seinfeld" Aptitude Test
Star Fleet Entrance Exam
The Star Trek Concordance
1201 Toughest TV Trivia
  Questions
What's Your "Frasier" IQ?
What's Your "Mad About You"
  IQ?

For a free full-color Entertainment Books brochure including the Citadel Film Series in depth and more, call 1-800-447-BOOK; or send your name and address to Citadel Film Books, Dept. 1598, 120 Enterprise Ave., Secaucus, NJ 07094.